STOP OVERTHINKING
STOP WORRYING

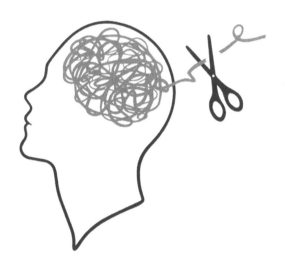

OVERCOME NEGATIVE THINKING WITH EASY EXERCISES AND
MASTER YOUR EMOTIONS TO ACHIEVE PEACE OF MIND

TONY RUELL

STOP OVERTHINKING, STOP WORRYING © Copyright 2023

All rights reserved.

TABLE OF CONTENTS

Introduction

Have you ever felt overwhelmed by your thoughts? Have you ever felt that your mind never stopped talking, analyzing, judging? If the answer is yes, you are in good company. Overthinking is a common problem for many people, and it can cause anxiety, stress, and even depression.

Our brains are designed to think, analyze, and predict, but when our minds become too noisy, it can be difficult to focus, make decisions, and enjoy the present moment. Overthinking can lead to a spiral of negativity, and a distorted sense of reality. Instead of seeing things as they are, we focus on our thoughts and worries, thus fueling our anxieties and insecurities.

But all is not lost. There are practical techniques and exercises that can help you free your mind from negative and depowering thoughts. This book aims to provide you with a wide range of tools you can use to regain control of your mind and enjoy life more peacefully and happily.

You will learn to identify negative thoughts, limiting beliefs and emotions that drag you down, and then use meditation techniques, mindfulness, breathing, self-compassion, gratitude, creativity and visualization to free yourself from these thoughts.

This book is not a magic solution to all your problems, but it offers a set of tools you can use to improve your quality of life and learn how to manage your thinking more effectively.

If you are ready to rid your mind of negative and depowering thoughts, start by reading this book. I hope you will find the exercises and techniques useful and be able to integrate them into your daily life to achieve the desired results.

Chapter 1.
The Mind, and the Power of Thought

The human mind is one of the most complex and fascinating structures in the universe. It enables us to think, imagine, dream, and reason. The mind manages our behavior, personality, and emotions. Therefore, understanding how the mind works is essential to understand how we act, and how we react to the world around us.

The mind can be divided into two main parts: (1) the conscious mind, and (2) the subconscious mind. The conscious mind allows us to think rationally and make conscious decisions. It is the part we use when we are awake and alert. The subconscious mind acts outside our awareness. It manages our automatic behavior and emotional reactions.

The subconscious mind is very powerful and can influence our behavior. It oversees many of our habits, emotions, and perceptions. In addition, the subconscious mind can be influenced by external factors (e.g., past experiences, suggestions, and beliefs).

One of the most interesting aspects of the subconscious mind is that it does not distinguish between reality and fantasy. This means that the subconscious mind can be influenced by images, sounds and thoughts that are processed in the conscious mind. This can be useful if you want to change your behavior, for example, to overcome a fear or negative habit.

In general, the subconscious mind is much more powerful than the conscious mind, but it often acts automatically and not rationally. This means that if we want to change our behavior, we need to work on the subconscious mind, using specific techniques to change our beliefs and thought patterns.

Thus, understanding how the mind works is essential to understanding our behavior and emotions. The conscious and subconscious minds are two interconnected parts of the mind that work together to determine our behavior. Understanding these two parts of the mind and how they interact with each other is an important step in being able to modify one's behavior and achieve one's goals.

The Role of Thought

The mind is a complex network of thoughts, emotions and behaviors that interact with each other to create our life experience. The role of thoughts in the mind is crucial, as they are the basis from which our emotions and behaviors arise. When we think about something, our brains process a range of information that allows us to interpret and understand the world around us. These thoughts may be positive or negative, rational or irrational, realistic or unrealistic, but they all have an impact on our experience of life.

Thoughts can generate specific emotions and behaviors because they are closely linked to our emotional system. When we have a negative thought, for example, our body responds with a negative emotion, such as anxiety, fear or sadness. This emotional response in turn can affect our behavior, such as causing social withdrawal or an angry reaction. In this way, our thoughts can have a cascading effect that affects the way we live and relate to others.

Conversely, positive thoughts can generate positive emotions, such as joy, gratitude or serenity, which in turn can lead to positive behaviors such as cooperation, help or enthusiasm. In this way, our thoughts can also influence our ability to pursue our goals, overcome difficulties and live a fulfilling life.

Therefore, it is important to understand how our thoughts work and how we can influence them to improve our quality of life. When we become aware of our thoughts and emotions, we can begin to change the negative thought patterns that limit us and make us anxious or depressed. We can learn to replace our negative thoughts with positive, rational and realistic ones that help us develop an open, flexible and positive mind.

In conclusion, thoughts play a crucial role in our life experience and can influence our behavior significantly. Understanding how our thoughts work and how we can influence them in a positive way can help us live happier and more fulfilling lives.

Automatic Thoughts

Automatic thoughts are generated in our minds without our awareness. These thoughts can be positive or negative, but those that negatively influence our behavior appear most often.

When we are stressed or worried, our automatic thoughts tend to be negative. For example, we may think, "I will never make it," "I am useless," "Everything is going wrong," etc. These thoughts can influence our behavior and lead us to give up or avoid certain situations that scare us or make us feel insecure.

However, it is important to understand that our thoughts are not reality, but only our interpretation of it. We can choose to replace negative automatic thoughts with positive ones to improve our mood and behavior.

To replace negative automatic thoughts with positive ones, we must first identify our negative thought patterns. There are several ways to do this, such as keeping a thought diary.

Once we have identified our negative thought patterns, we need to try to replace them with positive thoughts. For example, instead of thinking "I will never succeed," we can think "I can succeed if I try," instead of thinking "I am useless," we can think "I have many qualities that make me special."

In addition, it is important to note that negative automatic thoughts are often based on limiting beliefs, which are argued in the next chapter. Replacing negative automatic thoughts with positive ones can be a first step in changing our limiting beliefs and improving our mood and behavior.

In summary, automatic thoughts are those thoughts that are automatically generated in our minds without our awareness. These thoughts can influence our behavior in a negative way if they are negative. Replacing negative automatic thoughts with positive ones can help us improve our mood and behavior and can be a first step in changing our limiting beliefs.

Neuroplasticity

"Neuroplasticity" is a term used to describe the brain's ability to change and adapt in response to our experiences. Neural connections in the brain can be strengthened or weakened, depending on how the brain is used. Neuroplasticity is important for brain growth and development, but it can also be used to change unwanted behaviors and thoughts.

Practicing positive thoughts can affect the neuroplasticity of the brain in a positive way. When a person repeatedly thinks positive thoughts, such as feeling happy and grateful for one's life, the neural connections associated with those thoughts become stronger. As a result, it is easier for the person to continue thinking those positive thoughts in the future.

Neuroplasticity can also be used to change negative thoughts and behaviors. For example, if a person tends to automatically experience negative thoughts when a difficult situation arises, they can use neuroplasticity to disrupt this mental pattern and replace it with positive thoughts. This can be done by practicing positive thoughts and training the mind to focus on different thoughts.

Another way to use neuroplasticity to change negative thoughts and behaviors is by practicing mindfulness. Mindfulness is paying attention to the present moment without judging or reacting to any thoughts that occur. Mindfulness practice can help a person become aware of their automatic thought patterns and interrupt them to replace them with more positive thoughts.

In addition, neuroplasticity can be used to create new positive behavioral habits. When a person repeatedly practices a positive behavior, such as exercising or eating healthy, the neural connections associated with that behavior become stronger. As a result, the behavior becomes more automatic and easier to maintain over time.

In summary, neuroplasticity is an important feature of the brain that can be used to change unwanted thoughts and behaviors. Practicing positive thoughts and mindfulness are two ways in which neuroplasticity can be used to change negative thoughts and improve mental well-being. In addition, neuroplasticity can be used to create new positive behavioral habits.

The Law of Attraction

The law of attraction is a metaphysical principle in which one's thoughts and emotions have a direct impact on the physical world around them. This theory suggests that the external world reflects what a person thinks and feels, and therefore can be shaped with thought management. In other words, the law of attraction states that reality is a direct manifestation of our thoughts and emotions.

According to the law of attraction, if a person focuses on positive thoughts, then they will attract positive experiences into their life. Conversely, if a person focuses on negative thoughts, then they will attract negative experiences into their life. The law of attraction is based on the idea that people can attract what they want in life simply by focusing on their desires and believing they can achieve them.

The law of attraction has been the subject of scientific debate and popular opinion in recent years. Some argue that there is no scientific evidence to prove the existence of this law, while others believe that it is possible to use the law of attraction to improve one's life.

In any case, there are some strategies that can help people apply the principles of the law of attraction in their lives. The first thing to do is to focus on one's desires and the positive thoughts associated with them. This can help people attract positive experiences into their lives.

In addition, it is important to create a positive, optimistic atmosphere around you. Keep an open, positive mind and avoid focusing on negative, limiting thoughts.

Finally, it is important that people truly believe in their desires and the possibility of achieving them. Confidence and the belief that it is possible to achieve what one wants are fundamental to the application of the law of attraction.

In summary, the law of attraction states that one's thoughts and emotions have a direct impact on the physical world around them. Although there is debate about the scientific validity of this theory, many people believe it is possible to use the law of attraction to improve one's life. By focusing on your desires, creating a positive atmosphere around you, and believing in the possibility of achieving your goals, you can attract positive experiences into your life.

The Power of Language

The language we use can profoundly affect the way we think and act. In fact, the words we choose to use can have a great impact on our mental state and actions. For example, if we use negative and limiting words, we may end up feeling discouraged and powerless, while if we use positive and motivating words, we may feel more confident and motivated.

Positive affirmations are some of the most powerful ways to use language. Affirmations are phrases that describe a positive reality we wish to create. They can be used to replace negative thoughts with positive, motivating thoughts. For example, if you are facing a difficult situation, you might use an affirmation such as, "I am strong and determined, and I can overcome any obstacle that stands in my way."

In addition, the way we talk to others can affect the way we feel, and the way others see us. If we speak aggressively or critically, then we may end up alienating people and creating negative relationships. On the other hand, if we speak positively or constructively, then we can create positive and constructive relationships.

In addition, the way we talk about ourselves can have a great impact on our mental state. If we talk about ourselves in a negative and critical way, we may end up feeling depressed and insecure. On the other hand, if we talk about ourselves in a positive and motivating way, we may feel more confident and motivated.

In general, the power of language can be used to create a happier and more fulfilling life. Choosing positive and motivating words can help replace negative thoughts with positive and constructive ones, improve interpersonal relationships, and increase self-confidence.

Chapter 2.
Identifying Negative Thoughts

Our mind is a complex and fascinating place that allows us to think, imagine and dream. However, sometimes our thoughts can become a source of suffering, preventing us from fully enjoying life. Negative thoughts, such as fears, worries, doubts and regrets, can negatively affect our mental health, leading us to feel anxious, depressed or unmotivated. It is therefore important to learn to identify these thoughts in order to replace them with positive ones and improve our quality of life.

Identifying negative thoughts is the first step to addressing and overcoming them. Often, these thoughts recur and become a repeating pattern, thus creating a "mental cage" that prevents us from seeing things differently. Identifying these thought patterns is essential to break the cycle of negative thoughts.

Negative thoughts are often related to past or future events that may have hurt or worried us. This means that these thoughts are often linked to negative emotions, such as fear, anxiety, or guilt. However, negative thoughts can also be generated by low self-esteem or a distorted interpretation of reality.

Identifying negative thoughts is a process that takes time and practice. It is important to pay attention to our thoughts and emotions, trying to understand what is causing a particular thought or feeling. There are several techniques that can help identify negative thoughts, such as keeping a thought journal, meditating or talking to a mental health professional.

Once you have identified negative thoughts, you can replace

them with positive ones. This may seem difficult at first, especially if we are used to thinking negatively. However, there are techniques that can help change our thought patterns, which we will look at below.

To identify negative thoughts, it is important to understand how they manifest in our minds and how to recognize them. Negative thoughts can take many forms, from the more obvious and conscious to the more subtle and insidious ones that influence our behavior without us even realizing it.

One of the most common forms in which negative thoughts manifest themselves is self-criticism.

This can include thoughts such as:

- *"I'm stupid."*
- *"I'm not good enough."*
- *"I can't do it."*
- *"I don't deserve to be happy."*

These thoughts may be so ingrained in our minds that they seem true and justified, but they also represent a destructive way of thinking that can affect our behavior and our ability to make positive choices.

In addition, negative thoughts can also be expressed through anxiety and worry. We may worry about future situations and imagine catastrophic scenarios, which can lead to feelings of anxiety and stress. These thoughts can be so strong and compelling that they prevent us from dealing with situations in a positive and constructive way.

In some cases, negative thoughts may be so subtle that they are not immediately recognizable. For example, we may be critical of others, thinking that they are doing something wrong or letting us down. This kind of thinking can affect our behavior and interpersonal relationships, but it can be difficult to detect because it seems justified.

It is important to note that negative thoughts are not necessarily "wrong," but can be influenced by our experience, our environment, and our personal beliefs. However, recognizing negative thoughts is the first step in replacing them with more positive and constructive thoughts.

In summary, negative thoughts can manifest in a variety of ways and can affect our behavior in subtle or overt ways. Recognizing these thoughts is an important step in improving our mental health and psychological well-being.

Automatic Negative Thoughts

Automatic negative thoughts are thoughts that occur in our minds automatically and without any awareness. These thoughts can be caused by many things, such as past experiences, inner beliefs, thought patterns, emotions, stress, anxiety and depression. Negative automatic thoughts can have a negative impact on our mental health, as they can affect our mood, self-esteem, and behavior.

Negative automatic thoughts can be difficult to identify because they occur so automatically and subtly that we are often unaware of them. We can recognize negative automatic thoughts by observing our thoughts and emotions, particularly when we feel sad, angry or anxious for no apparent reason. In addition, we can pay attention to our thought patterns and inner beliefs that might influence our thoughts.

It is important to identify negative automatic thoughts because they can have a negative impact on our mental health. When we encounter a negative automatic thought, we often react emotionally without giving it much thought, which can lead to self-destructive behaviors such as isolation, avoidance of situations, or drug or alcohol use. These behaviors, in turn, can cause further negative thoughts and create a vicious cycle.

There are several techniques we can use to replace negative automatic thoughts with positive thoughts. One of the most effective techniques is to identify the negative thought, analyze it critically and replace it with a positive thought. For example, if we think "I am not good enough to do this job," we can replace it with "I have the skills to do this job and I will learn whatever it takes to do it well."

Another technique is to use diaphragmatic breathing, which helps reduce stress and increase awareness. Diaphragmatic breathing involves breathing slowly and deeply from the diaphragm, focusing attention on the breath and the movement of the diaphragm. This technique can help reduce negative thoughts and restore inner calm.

In conclusion, automatic negative thoughts are thoughts that arise in our mind automatically and without any awareness. These thoughts can have a negative impact on our mental health, affecting our mood, self-esteem and behavior. Identifying negative automatic thoughts is important to replace them with positive thoughts and to break the vicious cycle of negative thoughts and self-destructive behavior. There are many techniques we can use to replace negative automatic thoughts with positive thoughts and improve our lives.

Effects of Negative Thoughts

Negative thoughts have a significant impact on our mental health and behavior. When we are dominated by negative thoughts, we can feel anxious, stressed, and sometimes depressed. These effects can be debilitating and affect our ability to make decisions. In this section, we will explore how negative thoughts can affect our mental health and behavior.

Anxiety is one of the most common results of negative thoughts. When we are worried or anxious, we often struggle to concentrate and keep calm. This can have a negative impact on our daily lives, as we may not feel well enough to perform the activities that we are accustomed to. Anxiety can also manifest itself through physical symptoms (e.g., palpitations, sweating, and shortness of breath).

Stress is another common side effect of negative thoughts. When we are stressed, our bodies are in a constant state of alarm, and this can affect our physical and mental health. Chronic stress can lead to long-term health problems (e.g., high blood pressure and heart failure). In addition, stress can affect our ability to sleep, which can further impair our mental health.

Depression is another common effect of negative thoughts. When we feel depressed, we may lose interest in activities we once enjoyed, and have difficulty focusing on work and daily life. Depression can also lead to physical health problems, such as heart and immune problems.

Negative thoughts can also affect our ability to make decisions. When we are overwhelmed by negative thoughts, it becomes difficult to see things objectively. We feel overwhelmed and confused, and this can lead to greater indecision and difficulty in making important decisions. In addition, negative thoughts can lead to selective attention, which means that we focus only on the negative aspects of a situation and ignore the positive ones.

In conclusion, negative thoughts have a significant impact on our mental health and behavior. When we are overwhelmed by negative thoughts, we may feel anxious, stressed and sometimes depressed. In addition, negative thoughts can affect our ability to make decisions and see things objectively. Identifying and replacing negative thoughts with positive thoughts can have a significant impact on our mental health and overall well-being.

How to Replace Negative Thoughts with Positive Thoughts

Replacing negative thoughts with positive thoughts is an important process for improving our mental health and psychological well-being. However, it can be difficult to identify one's negative thoughts and replace them with positive thoughts, especially when these thoughts are automatic and not conscious.

The first thing to do is become aware of your negative thoughts. Once identified, you can replace them with positive thoughts using positive affirmations, which are short, simple phrases to repeat to yourself in place of your negative thoughts. For example, if you have a negative thought (e.g., "I am not good enough for this job"), then you can replace it with a positive affirmation (e.g., "I am capable and have the skills to do this job.")

Another useful strategy is to reflect on one's successes and strengths. By focusing on what we have done well in the past, we can create positive thoughts and increase our self-esteem. In this way, we can also overcome future difficulties with greater self-confidence.

Another technique for replacing negative thoughts with positive thoughts is to use imagination. We can imagine being in a positive situation and repeat positive statements to ourselves in relation to that situation. For example, if we are facing a difficult exam, we can imagine that we are successful and repeat to ourselves statements such as "I am prepared and I know I can succeed."

Finally, it is important to remember that replacing negative thoughts with positive thoughts does not mean ignoring real problems. It is important to recognize difficulties and seek concrete solutions to address them. Replacing negative thoughts with positive thoughts is just one strategy to improve our mental health and psychological well-being.

In summary, replacing negative thoughts with positive thoughts takes time and practice, but it can have a significant impact on our mental health and psychological well-being. It is important to become aware of one's negative thoughts, use positive affirmations, reflect on one's successes and strengths, use imagination, and remember to address real problems.

The Importance of Positive Self-Talk

Positive self-talk is a mental habit of using positive words and expressions when thinking or talking about oneself. This practice can have a significant impact on an individual's mental health and psychological well-being.

Positive self-talk is often associated with self-esteem since the words we use to describe ourselves affect our self-perception. If we talk about ourselves negatively, then we tend to perceive ourselves as "inferior" and "less capable." However, if we use positive, constructive words, then we tend to feel more confident and self-satisfied.

Positive self-talk can also influence our motivation. When we talk about ourselves positively, we feel more motivated to achieve our goals and face any challenges we meet along the way. However, if we talk about ourselves negatively, then we tend to feel unmotivated and unsure of our abilities.

In addition, positive self-talk can help us cope with difficulties. When we are faced with a difficult or stressful situation, the words we use to describe the situation can affect our ability to cope with it. If we speak negatively to each other, we tend to perceive the situation as insurmountable and feel helpless. On the other hand, if we use positive and constructive words, we tend to perceive the situation as a challenge that we can face and overcome.

To develop the habit of positive self-talk, it is important to pay attention to the words we use to describe ourselves and talk to others. When you realize that you are using negative or limiting words, you can try to replace them with positive and constructive words. For example, instead of saying "I am not good enough for this," you can say "I can do my best and learn to improve."

In addition, it is helpful to remember to focus on one's strengths and successes achieved, rather than focusing only on mistakes or failures. The goal of positive self-talk is not to deny problems or difficulties, but to deal with them constructively and to develop a positive perspective on one's life and abilities.

In conclusion, positive self-talk can have a significant impact on mental health and psychological well-being. Replacing negative thoughts with positive words and expressions can help improve self-esteem, motivation and coping.

Practical Exercises to Identify and Replace Negative Thoughts

There are many practical exercises that can help identify and replace negative thoughts with positive ones. One of the first steps is self-observation, which involves paying attention to one's thoughts and the emotions these thoughts generate. In this way, you can identify negative thoughts and limiting beliefs that may influence our behavior.

Another useful exercise is the practice of gratitude. This exercise involves being aware of the positive things that happen in our lives and expressing gratitude for these things. This can help focus on the positives in life and increase the sense of well-being and gratitude.

A third exercise is replacing negative thoughts with positive thoughts. This exercise involves identifying negative thoughts and replacing them with positive thoughts. For example, if you have the thought "I am not good enough," you can replace it with "I am capable and have achieved many successes in my life."

A fourth exercise is to be kind to yourself. We often treat ourselves more harshly than we treat others. The exercise of kindness is to treat ourselves as kindly and understandingly as we treat others.

A fifth exercise is to be present in the present moment. Often negative thoughts are related to the past or future and can prevent us from experiencing the present moment. Being aware of the present can help us focus on the positive things happening in the present moment.

In summary, there are many practical exercises that can help identify and replace negative thoughts with positive ones.

These exercises can be used in daily life to improve mental health and psychological well-being. The important thing is to practice these exercises regularly and adapt them to your own needs and circumstances.

Chapter 3.
Reducing Your Limiting Beliefs

Limiting beliefs are assumptions we make about the world, others, and ourselves that prevent us from reaching our potential. Often, these assumptions are made unconsciously, and we do not realize how they affect the way we think and perceive reality. In this chapter, we will focus on identifying these beliefs and presenting strategies to overcome them.

Limiting beliefs may stem from negative experiences we have had in the past, messages we have received since childhood, cultural stereotypes, and other factors. For example, a person who was bullied in school might develop the limiting belief that they are not good enough or worthy of love and respect. This limiting belief might then influence their adult life, thus leading them to self-sabotage situations that require self-confidence.

Limiting beliefs can also manifest themselves as negative automatic thoughts that run through our minds. For example, a person who does not feel confident in public might automatically think "I am not good enough" or "Everyone judges me." These automatic thoughts are often irrational and unrealistic, but they can have a significant impact on our mood and actions.

Working on limiting beliefs requires identifying them and examining whether they are realistic or not. Sometimes, a limiting belief may have a kernel of truth, but it may be exaggerated or applied inappropriately. For example, a person who has made a mistake at work may automatically think, "I am a total failure," when in fact the mistake is only an isolated incident and does not mean that the person is an absolute failure.

Once we have identified our limiting beliefs, we can replace them with more positive and realistic beliefs. This can take time and effort, but it can have a significant impact on our lives. We can also seek the support of a therapist or coach to help us in this process.

In summary, limiting beliefs prevent us from reaching our potential. These beliefs may stem from negative experiences or irrational automatic thoughts. Identifying and overcoming these limiting beliefs can take time and effort but can also help us live more satisfying and fulfilling lives.

Identifying Your Limiting Beliefs

Identifying limiting beliefs is the first step to break free from them and change the way we perceive reality. Limiting beliefs are thoughts that prevent us from achieving our goals and adversely affect our daily lives. They are often rooted in our subconscious, and we are often unaware of their impact on our lives.

To identify limiting beliefs, it is important to pay attention to the signs that reveal their presence. One of the first signs is the presence of self-sabotage. When we self-sabotage, we place unconscious obstacles in our way that prevent us from achieving our goals. This may manifest itself through avoidance of situations that frighten or challenge us, or through self-criticism and feeling that we are not up to the task.

Another sign that may indicate the presence of limiting beliefs is the tendency to generalize experiences. For example, if we have failed in a specific situation, we may generalize that failure to all future situations, thus developing a limiting belief that prevents us from trying again.

Fear of the unknown is another sign that may indicate the

presence of limiting beliefs. Limiting beliefs keep us safe in our comfort zone, preventing us from experiencing and growing as individuals. If we fear change or uncertainty, we may have limiting beliefs that prevent us from taking on new challenges.

Finally, another sign that may indicate the presence of limiting beliefs is the presence of self-judgment. When we judge ourselves harshly, we put ourselves in a position of weakness and prevent ourselves from reaching our full potential.

To identify limiting beliefs, it is important to pay attention to these signs and reflect on them. Thought journaling can be a useful tool for identifying limiting thoughts and assessing their impact on our lives. Once the limiting beliefs have been identified, you can start working on them to change them and free yourself from the limitations that prevent us from achieving our goals.

Causes of Limiting Beliefs

Limiting beliefs are thoughts we carry within us that prevent us from reaching our full potential. But how did these beliefs form? Many of our limiting beliefs develop during childhood and adolescence, when the experiences we have are still new and can affect our worldview.

The education we receive from our family, our teachers, and society in general plays a major role in the development of our limiting beliefs. For example, if we received negative messages as children about our ability to achieve certain goals or succeed in a certain field, it is likely that these limiting beliefs will continue to influence our thinking as adults.

Past experiences can also be a source of limiting beliefs. If we have had a bad experience in a certain situation, we may develop the belief that that situation is always bad, even if there is evidence to the contrary. For example, if we had a bad experience in a public presentation, we might develop the limiting belief that we are not good at public speaking.

The opinions of others may also contribute to the formation of our limiting beliefs. For example, if we are told by more than one person that we are not good at something, we may begin to believe that it is true, even if there is no evidence to confirm it.

In general, limiting beliefs develop due to a combination of factors, including upbringing, past experiences, and the opinions of others. However, it is important to remember that these beliefs are not necessarily true and that we can work on them to change them and reach our full potential.

How Limiting Beliefs Become Obstacles

Limiting beliefs can have a significant impact on our lives, affecting the way we act and think. When we believe in something that limits us, we put stakes in ourselves that can prevent us from achieving our goals and limit our actions. In this way, limiting beliefs can become an obstacle to our personal and professional development.

One of the most obvious consequences of limiting beliefs is the loss of self-esteem. When we believe we cannot do something, or we are not good enough, we feel less confident, and this can negatively affect our self-esteem. In addition, limiting beliefs can cause anxiety and a fear of failure. Often, people who have limiting beliefs tend to avoid situations that may lead to failure, thus forgoing new opportunities and limiting their potential.

Limiting beliefs can also lead to initiative blocking. When we believe we are unable to do something, we often do not even try. This leads us to miss many opportunities in life and become trapped in our comfort zone. In addition, limiting beliefs can affect the way we act and think, leading us to make ineffective or even counterproductive choices.

In conclusion, limiting beliefs have a significant impact on our lives and limit our potential. However, it is important to remember that limiting beliefs are only thoughts and do not necessarily reflect reality. We can work on these limiting beliefs by changing and overcoming them to unlock our potential and achieve our goals.

How to Change Your Limiting Beliefs

Once you have identified your limiting beliefs, you can work on them to transform them into more positive and functional beliefs. One of the most effective techniques is cognitive restructuring, which involves questioning limiting beliefs and trying to find evidence for or against them. For example, if you believe you are unable to meet a certain challenge, you can look for evidence to the contrary, such as past situations in which you were able to overcome similar obstacles.

Another technique is to replace limiting beliefs with more positive and functional beliefs. For example, if you believe you are not good at a certain activity, you can replace this belief with a more positive and realistic one, such as "I can improve with practice and commitment."

Positive affirmations can be another useful technique for replacing limiting beliefs. These are positive phrases that are repeated to oneself to create a new mental pattern. For example, one can repeat "I am capable and deserving of success" whenever one feels a negative thought related to one's ability to achieve results.

Finally, self-compassion can help work on one's limiting beliefs, as it allows one to accept one's imperfections and recognize that all human beings are subject to mistakes and limitations. The practice of mindfulness can be helpful in this regard, as it helps to become aware of one's thoughts and emotions, without judging or criticizing them.

In summary, there are several techniques and strategies that can be used to change one's limiting beliefs and improve one's mental well-being. Cognitive restructuring, replacing limiting beliefs with more positive and functional beliefs, positive affirmations, and practicing self-compassion are just some of the techniques that can be used for this purpose. The important thing is to have an awareness of one's limiting beliefs and a desire to work on them to achieve a more satisfying and fulfilling life.

Examples of Common Limiting Beliefs

Limiting beliefs are often unconscious and can significantly influence how we perceive ourselves and the world around us. Some of the most common limiting beliefs relate to one's competence, one's worth, and one's ability to love and be loved, but they may differ depending on one's experiences and personality.

One of the most common limiting beliefs is that "I am not good enough." This belief can affect the way we approach many situations, leading us not to try new activities or seek expert help for fear of failure or being judged. To transform this limiting belief into a more functional and positive one, one can adopt the strategy of cognitive restructuring, that is, replacing the negative belief with a positive one, for example, "I am good at some things and can improve at others."

Another common limiting belief is the belief that "I do not measure up." This belief can lead to a lack of self-confidence and a tendency to stay in the comfort zone, avoiding challenges and opportunities for growth. To transform this limiting belief, one can adopt the strategy of self-compassion, acknowledging one's limitations and accepting that making mistakes is part of the learning process.

A third common limiting belief is the belief that "I am unlovable." This belief can lead to low self-esteem and a tendency to relate defensively or aggressively to others. To transform this limiting belief, one can adopt the strategy of replacing limiting beliefs with more positive and functional beliefs, such as "I am lovable and appreciated for my unique qualities."

In general, to transform limiting beliefs into more functional, positive beliefs, it is important to do the following:

1. Adopt a more realistic and objective perspective
2. Recognize the evidence that supports your new belief
3. Practice your new belief regularly
4. Use positive affirmations to cement your new belief

Thus, limiting beliefs can have a significant impact on our lives and mental health, but through techniques and strategies such as cognitive restructuring, replacing limiting beliefs with more functional and positive beliefs, and using self-compassion, we can transform these beliefs so that we can live more satisfying and fuller lives.

Here are some other examples of common limiting beliefs:

• **"I'm not smart enough."** This limiting belief can lead to a fear of facing new challenges and avoiding situations that require a certain level of intelligence or competence. A transformation of this belief could be, **"I am always learning and can develop my intelligence with experience and training."**

• **"I don't deserve to be happy."** This limiting belief can lead to sabotaging relationships or depression. A transformation of this belief could be, **"I deserve to be happy, and I will work hard to create my own happiness."**

• **"I am not thin enough."** This limiting belief can lead to an obsession with dieting and exercise and can cause a distorted perception of one's body. A transformation of this belief could be, **"I love myself for who I am—regardless of my body shape—and I will take care of my body in a healthy and sustainable way."**

• **"I can't trust others."** This limiting belief can lead to difficulty making meaningful connections with others and a fear of being hurt or betrayed. A transformation of this belief could be, **"I can learn to trust others and be open to meaningful relationships."**

• **"I cannot manage stress."** This limiting belief can lead to a fear of stressful situations and a tendency to avoid conflict. A transformation of this belief could be, **"I can manage stress effectively and learn to cope with difficult situations calmly and resiliently."**

Constant Practice

Once you have identified your limiting beliefs, the main work is to transform them into more functional and positive beliefs. Importantly, this process takes time and constant practice.

Constant practice is the key to transforming your limiting beliefs. This means making minor progress each day to improve your mental well-being and achieve your goals. For example, you can start with making minor changes to your daily routine (e.g., repeating positive affirmations to yourself each morning) to encourage more positive, functional beliefs.

In conclusion, working on one's limiting beliefs is an ongoing process that requires constant commitment and dedication. Identifying one's limiting beliefs, using techniques to transform them into more functional and positive beliefs, and constant practice are essential elements in improving one's mental well-being and achieving one's goals.

Chapter 4.
The Thought Diary

This journal is a powerful tool to help identify recurring thoughts that limit us and make us anxious or depressed and to deal with them constructively.

Thought journaling is an activity that takes only a few minutes a day, but it can have a significant impact on your mental health and emotional well-being. To get started, choose a quiet moment and spend a few minutes writing down your negative thoughts.

The diary should contain the thoughts they repeat often in their minds, their emotions and their worries.

There are no strict rules on how to write the diary, but there are some tips that can be helpful for best results:

1. Choose a quiet time of day: the best time to journal your thoughts might be before going to bed or early in the morning, when the mind is still fresh and relaxed.

2. Write down thoughts without judgment: it is important to write down everything that comes to mind, even if it seems insignificant or silly. There is no judgment or evaluation of thoughts.

3. Write down the feelings associated with the thoughts: it is not enough to list negative thoughts. It is also important to write down the feelings that are associated with these thoughts. This will help you better understand your own emotions and thought patterns.

4. Try to be honest with yourself: the thought journal is a safe place where you can write down everything that goes through your mind. Try to be honest with yourself, even if your thoughts seem irrational or embarrassing.

5. Write regularly: it is important to write regularly in your thought journal. This will help identify recurring thoughts and monitor your progress.

Writing in a thought journal is an important activity that will reduce your obsessive thoughts and help you relax. It will also help you identify negative thoughts and the emotions that accompany them, thus allowing you to analyze them objectively. Once you have identified your negative thought patterns, you can replace them with positive, constructive thoughts.

Analyze Your Thoughts

I now invite you to carefully examine the negative thoughts listed in the thought journal and evaluate whether they are realistic, rational, and helpful or whether they are irrational, unrealistic, and unhelpful. The goal of this exercise is to help you become more aware of your own thoughts and understand how they may affect their mental health and well-being.

The first step to analyze your thoughts is to carefully read your thought journal and identify those thoughts that recur the most. Once these thoughts are identified, you can reflect on them and ask yourself whether they are realistic, rational, and useful—or whether they are irrational, unrealistic, and unhelpful.

For example, if a recurring negative thought is, *"I'm not good enough for this job,"* then you should consider whether this thought is realistic and rational—or whether it is simply the result of low self-esteem or excessive insecurities. In this case, it might be helpful to reflect on your skills and competencies, and how they relate to the job in question.

These self-reflection exercises can be used to help you understand your emotions, and how they affect your thoughts. For example, you can make a list of all the emotions you experience in a day and reflect on what triggered each of these emotions.

The goal is to help you become more aware of your thoughts and emotions so that you can better cope with difficult situations and free yourself from negative thoughts that can harm your mental well-being.

Challenge Negative Thoughts

The first step to challenging negative thoughts is to become aware of them. Once you have identified your limiting thoughts, it is important to create a rational response to them. For example, if you think, *"I'm not good enough,"* then you can challenge this thought by asking yourself, "Is this true? What are some things that I am good at? What are some results that I have achieved so far?"

Another effective technique to challenge negative thoughts is to replace them with positive, constructive thoughts. For example, instead of thinking, *"I will never succeed,"* you can replace this thought with, *"I can succeed if I put in the effort and work hard."* In this way, you can create a positive and constructive response to your limiting thoughts.

As mentioned above, it is important to keep track of their progress in replacing limiting thoughts with positive ones.

A practical example of how to challenge a negative thought might be the following:

• **Negative Thought:** *"I can never get things right."*

• Thought Analysis: Examine this thought and try to see whether it is realistic, rational, and useful—or whether it is irrational, unrealistic, and unhelpful. In this case, the thought is irrational and unrealistic because no one fails in every situation.

• Thought Challenge & Substitution: Challenge this negative thought by replacing it with a positive, realistic thought. For example, try thinking, "I may not have been successful at this specific task, but there are many other things I can do well!"

• Practical Exercise: Now, try to remember this new thought each time the old, negative thought comes into your mind so that you can gradually restructure the way you think by replacing negative thoughts with positive ones.

Below you can jot down your thoughts as outlined in this chapter.

_____

_____

_____

_____

_____

Chapter 5.
Self-Compassion Exercises

Self-compassion is a skill that enables one to treat oneself with kindness, warmth and affection when in distress, just as a close friend would. The practice of self-compassion has been widely studied and recognized as an effective technique for improving mental health and overall well-being.

Many people tend to criticize and judge themselves harshly when they make mistakes or when they find themselves in difficult situations. This behavior often leads to increased negative thoughts and negative moods, such as anxiety and depression. The practice of self-compassion offers a positive and constructive alternative to this behavior.

Being kind to yourself means accepting who you are, along with all your flaws and imperfections. Self-compassion will help you develop a positive view of yourself, as well as foster your self-esteem and self-confidence. It will also help you accept difficulties and disappointments more easily, as well as learn from them, instead of becoming overwhelmed by a sense of failure.

Scientific studies have shown that practicing self-compassion can reduce stress and anxiety, improve mood and sleep quality, and increase resilience and the ability to manage emotions. It can also help reduce self-criticism and judgment toward others, fostering greater understanding and connection with others.

In summary, self-compassion is a useful skill to clear the mind of negative thoughts. It helps you develop a positive view of yourself and manage difficulties easier. Regularly practicing self-compassion can lead to greater mental health and well-being.

The Importance of Self-Forgiveness

Self-forgiveness is a crucial step to self-compassion. Often, when we make a mistake or do not meet our own expectations, we judge and criticize ourselves harshly, instead of being kind and understanding to ourselves. These negative thoughts and behaviors can lead to a worse mental state and can be detrimental to our health. Therefore, it is essential to learn to forgive ourselves.

Self-forgiveness is the act of releasing self-judgment and self-blame for mistakes and/or poor choices we have made. This does not mean we should minimize the severity of our actions or justify our harmful behavior, but we should accept that we all make mistakes, and excessive self-criticism serves no one.

To learn how to forgive yourself, first identify the situations or events that cause you the most stress and make you turn to self-criticism. Next, examine your own unrealistic expectations or judgments and try to replace them with more compassionate thoughts. For example, if you criticize yourself harshly when you do not achieve a goal, then remind yourself that we all fail sometimes, and this does not make you any less deserving of respect and kindness.

Another way to learn to forgive ourselves is through the practice of mindfulness. Mindfulness helps us become more aware of our thoughts and feelings without judging them or reacting to them automatically. In this way, we can develop greater understanding and compassion for ourselves and others.

Finally, we can also consider the importance of apologizing and making amends when necessary. Apologizing can be a way to show our understanding of the pain or harm we have caused others and to demonstrate our commitment to improvement. This can also help us rid ourselves of the sense of guilt and repentance that may prevent us from forgiving ourselves.

In conclusion, learning to forgive ourselves is a crucial step in self-compassion and liberation from negativity and obsessive thoughts. This requires constant practice and a willingness to accept our humanity and failures. With practice and perseverance, we can develop greater kindness and understanding for ourselves and others, improving our overall well-being and mental health.

How to Avoid Self-Criticism and Judgment

Self-criticism and judgment toward oneself can be two of the main factors that fuel negative thoughts in the mind. We often find ourselves criticizing our past actions or choices and judging ourselves harshly for who we are or what we have done. This attitude can lead to a feeling of inadequacy and dissatisfaction in life.

To avoid self-criticism and judgment, it is important to become aware of our negative tendencies and how they may affect our lives. One of the first things we can do is to pay attention to our thoughts and try to identify those that criticize or judge us.

Once you become aware of these thoughts, you can replace them with more positive, kinder thoughts. For example, instead of criticizing your physical appearance, you can focus on something positive about yourself (e.g., your sense of humor). You can also learn to become more tolerant of your past actions by understanding that mistakes are opportunities to gain experience and grow, not a reason to judge yourself.

Another way to avoid self-criticism and judgment is to develop self-compassion. Self-compassion consists of treating oneself with the same kind of kindness, care and support that we would offer to a friend who is going through a difficult time.

To develop self-compassion, you can practice compassion meditation, which will help you cultivate self-love and kindness. You can also talk to yourself in the same way that you would talk to a good friend, by using kind and encouraging words to self-motivate.

Finally, to avoid self-criticism and judgment, it is important to learn to look at situations from different perspectives. We often criticize or judge ourselves because we see only one side of a situation. Learning to see things from a different perspective helps us understand the situation better and be kinder to ourselves.

In summary, avoiding self-criticism and judgment is important to free the mind from negative thoughts. We can become more aware of our negative tendencies, develop self-compassion and look at situations from different perspectives to avoid judging ourselves and to learn to be kinder and more compassionate toward ourselves.

The Importance of Self-Help

Self-support is a skill that can be developed to learn how to support oneself during difficult times. Being able to provide oneself with the necessary support can be an important step in self-compassion, as it allows us to feel less alone and more able to cope.

There are many self-help techniques that can help calm your mind and allow you to feel more in control of your emotions. Meditation is a common technique that can be practiced anywhere, at any time of day. Even as little as 10 minutes of meditation a day can help reduce stress and increase mind-and-body awareness.

Another useful technique is visualization, which involves imagining a relaxing or positive situation. For example, if you are experiencing anxiety, you can imagine yourself at a quiet beach, feeling the sound of the waves and the wind on your face. This technique can help distract your mind from negative thoughts and help you feel calmer.

Self-massage can be another useful self-help technique to get rid of negative thoughts. Even just gently massaging your hands or face can help you relax and decrease muscle tension.

To develop a sense of self-support, it is also important to learn how to take care of ourselves physically and mentally. This means eating healthy and nutritious foods, getting enough sleep, exercising regularly and devoting time to hobbies and activities we enjoy.

In addition, it is important to learn to ask for help when we need it. Asking for support from friends or family members can be an important step in self-compassion, as it allows us to feel less alone and share the burden of our worries.

In conclusion, developing a sense of self-support can be an important step in self-compassion. It is also important to learn to take care of ourselves physically and mentally, and to ask friends or family for support when we need it.

How to Cultivate Self-Compassion

Cultivating self-compassion requires constant practice and patience, but the benefits it brings are invaluable to mental health and overall well-being. In this section, we will explore some practical exercises that you can use to cultivate self-compassion.

The loving kindness meditation is one of the most effective exercises for cultivating self-compassion. This meditation is based on sending messages of kindness and love to yourself and others. To begin, sit in a quiet, comfortable place. Close your eyes and focus on your breathing for a few moments. Then, begin to visualize yourself and repeat phrases to yourself such as "May I be happy," "May I be free from pain and suffering," "May I feel love and kindness from myself." These phrases can be customized to suit individual needs.

Another exercise that can be helpful in cultivating self-compassion is to write a letter of kindness to yourself. Sit down in a quiet, comfortable place and take some time to reflect on your past experiences and the ways you treated yourself in those situations. Then, write a kindness letter to yourself, listing your positive qualities and the things you appreciate about yourself. Also include messages of support and encouragement for any future difficulties you may face.

Finally, another exercise that can help cultivate self-compassion is visualizing a support figure. Imagine a support figure in your life, which could be a real or imaginary person. Visualize this support figure sending you messages of kindness and support, such as "You are a wonderful person" or "You deserve to be loved." Imagine this support figure hugging you and reassuring you.

In conclusion, consistently practicing self-compassion can help you develop a kinder attitude, freeing yourself from negative thoughts, and promote your mental and physical well-being. Experimenting with different self-compassion techniques and finding the one that works best for you may take some time, but the investment will be worth it!

How to Integrate Self-Compassion into Your Daily Life

Self-compassion is a skill that can be cultivated and integrated into daily life. Many people find it difficult to maintain a compassionate attitude toward themselves, especially in times of stress or difficulty. However, there are several strategies that can help integrate self-compassion into daily life.

One way to integrate self-compassion into daily life is through self-reflection. This means taking the time to reflect on one's thoughts and feelings, and trying to understand how they affect one's well-being. One can use meditation or mindfulness techniques to become more aware of one's thoughts and emotions.

In addition, relaxation techniques can help integrate self-compassion into daily life. These may include breathing, stretching or yoga exercises. The goal of these techniques is to reduce stress and muscle tension, and to promote a sense of calm and relaxation.

Another strategy for integrating self-compassion into daily life is to find ways to practice self-compassion in specific situations. For example, if you are going through a difficult time, you can try to be kind and compassionate to yourself instead of self-criticizing or judging yourself harshly. One can use self-compassion phrases such as "I accept myself as I am" or "I deserve love and respect."

In addition, it is important to try to create a positive supportive environment around oneself. This may include seeking support from friends and family, attending support groups, or finding a therapist who can help develop self-compassion.

In conclusion, integrating self-compassion into daily life takes time and effort. However, the benefits of this skill can be significant for mental health and overall well-being. By using self-reflection, relaxation and self-compassion techniques in specific situations, one can develop a kinder and more compassionate mind toward oneself and others.

Chapter 6.
The Importance of Focusing on the Present Moment

Mindfulness in the present moment, also known as mindfulness, is a practice that helps us focus on the here and now. It consists of being aware of our thoughts, emotions and physical sensations without judging them or automatically reacting to them. In this chapter, we will explore some mindfulness exercises that can help you achieve these goals.

Mindfulness has been associated with numerous mental health benefits, including reducing stress, anxiety and depression. It also helps develop resilience and the ability to cope more effectively with life's difficulties.

Mindfulness can help clear the mind of negative thoughts by allowing us to distance ourselves from them. Often, when we acknowledge our negative thoughts, we allow ourselves to be overwhelmed by the negative emotions that accompany them. Mindfulness helps us observe these thoughts without judgment or automatically reacting to them, which allows us to develop a greater awareness of what is happening in our minds and bodies.

There are several techniques for practicing mindfulness, including meditation, mindful breathing and observing our thoughts and feelings. Activities such as yoga, tai chi and mindful walking can also be helpful in developing mindfulness.

For many, the practice of mindfulness may seem difficult or unfamiliar at first. However, with practice and perseverance, mindfulness can become a natural part of daily life, helping us to maintain a positive mind and get rid of the negative thoughts that often plague us.

The Difference Between the Past, Present, and Future

The past and the future can be sources of worry and anxiety for many people. People may get stuck in the past, constantly rethinking their mistakes or regretting missed opportunities. Conversely, people may also be worried about the future, anxious about the challenges they will face or the possibility of failure.

Focusing on the present moment, however, invites us to focus on the here and now. It helps us become aware of the present and enjoy the moments we are experiencing. This means accepting the past for what it is, recognizing that the future is uncertain and focusing on the present moment.

To maintain a positive mind, it is important that we focus on the present moment. When we are focused on the past or the future, we miss out on the experience of the present and miss the opportunity to appreciate the beauty of life. When we focus on the present, we become more aware of our thoughts, emotions and actions.

Several techniques can keep your focus on the present moment. For example, meditation and mindfulness can help you focus on the present moment and reduce stress and anxiety. Meditation can also help create an inner space, where your mind can rest and recover.

In addition to meditation, there are other techniques that can help keep the focus on the present moment. For example, art and music can be used as means to focus on the present moment and find inner peace. Daily activities, such as eating or washing, can also be used as opportunities to focus on the present moment.

In summary, the mind can become a dangerous place when we focus too much on the past or the future. Focusing on the present moment can help keep a positive mind focused on the present, freeing us from negative thoughts and bringing peace and happiness into our daily lives.

How to Stay Present During Your Daily Activities

Keeping the focus on the present moment during daily activities can seem challenging, especially in a world where we are constantly bombarded with distractions. However, it can be an effective way to rid the mind of negative thoughts and maintain a positive mind.

For example, many people tend to eat distractedly, while checking their phones or watching TV. This can lead to a lack of awareness or satisfaction from the food being eaten. Instead, take the time to sit and eat mindfully, while observing the flavors and textures of the food to focus your attention on the present moment and avoid negative thoughts.

In addition, even seemingly mundane activities such as walking or showering can be used as moments to practice attention to the present moment. When walking, for example, one can focus on the sounds of nature or the feeling of feet touching the ground. In the shower, on the other hand, one can pay attention to the temperature of the water and the feel of the water on the skin.

These moments can become "rituals" for practicing mindfulness and maintaining a positive mind. When you realize you are distracted by negative thoughts, you can focus on breathing and try to bring your attention back to the present moment, rediscovering the beauty of small things.

In general, keeping the focus on the present moment requires practice and perseverance. But once you acquire the ability to stay present and mindful, you can experience an increase in mental well-being and a greater ability to face daily challenges with a positive mind.

How to Avoid Distractions and Stop Multitasking

In modern society, distraction and multitasking have become common elements of daily life. With the advent of smartphones, tablets, and laptops, it is easy to become distracted by notifications, emails, and text messages. In addition, the culture of always being busy leads many people to multitask, that is, to do several things at once.

However, distraction and multitasking can fuel negative thoughts and increase stress. When people focus on multiple things at once, it is easy to become overwhelmed and feel overwhelmed by their thoughts. Instead, focusing on the present moment can help reduce stress and maintain a positive mind.

There are several strategies people can use to avoid distraction and multitasking. First, it is important to limit the time spent on digital devices. This can be done by setting time limits for phone or computer use, or keeping devices out of sight when they are not needed.

Second, people can focus on only one activity at a time, avoiding jumping from one thing to another. This can help reduce stress and improve productivity. In addition, people can use breathing or meditation techniques to help them focus on one activity and stay present in the moment.

Finally, it is important to take time to relax and rest your mind. This can be done through meditation, yoga, reading or other activities that help you relax and get rid of negative thoughts.

Thus, focusing on the present moment can be an important strategy to rid the mind of negative thoughts and maintain a positive mind. Avoiding distraction and multitasking can be an effective way to stay present and focus on one activity at a time. This can help reduce stress and increase mental well-being.

Here are some practical examples of how to avoid distraction and multitasking:

• While you are talking to someone, avoid checking notifications on your phone or doing other activities at the same time. Devote your time and attention to the conversation.

• While you are working on a project, turn off your phone and computer notifications and focus only on your task. If necessary, you can schedule a time interval in which to check your email or notifications.

• While you are eating, avoid watching TV or reading the newspaper. Instead, take the time to enjoy the food and appreciate the flavors.

• While you are walking, avoid listening to music or looking at your phone. Focus on your senses, and the sensations in your body as you walk.

These are just a few examples, but there are many other activities where you can apply attention to the present moment and avoid distraction and multitasking.

How to Pay Attention to the Present Moment in Your Daily Life

Integrating the focus on the present moment into daily life can be a challenge for many people. As we have said, there are so many distractions in modern life that it is easy to lose sight of what is happening in the present moment. However, there are several strategies people can use to help themselves stay present during the day.

One of the most effective strategies is to practice mindfulness meditation. Mindfulness meditation involves focusing on the present experience, observing one's thoughts and feelings without judgment. There are several mindfulness meditation techniques that people can use, such as mindful breathing or body scanning. Mindfulness meditation can be practiced anywhere, from the park to the workplace.

Another strategy for integrating the focus on the present moment into daily life is to take a break and focus on your bodily sensations. This means taking a moment to focus on your breathing, tension in your muscles, or any other physical sensation. This can help interrupt negative thoughts and reconnect with the present moment.

Everyday activities such as walking or showering can also be turned into exercises in mindfulness about the present moment. For example, instead of letting the mind wander while walking, one can make a conscious effort to observe one's surroundings, noticing colors, sounds and smells. While taking a shower, instead of thinking about what to do next, one can focus on the feeling of the water on the skin.

Finally, it is important to minimize distraction and multitasking throughout the day. This means avoiding looking at your smartphone during meals, avoiding answering emails while working on an important project, and taking the time to complete only one task at a time. This can help reduce the feeling of mental overload and keep your focus on the present moment.

In general, integrating a focus on the present moment into daily life requires practice and perseverance. However, with regular use of techniques such as mindfulness meditation and reducing multitasking, people can learn to live in the present moment and face life with a more positive mind free from negative thoughts.

Mindfulness Exercises to Help You Pay Attention to the Present Moment

Mindfulness is awareness of the present moment and the acceptance of thoughts and emotions without judgment. Mindfulness practice can help clear the mind of negative thoughts and develop focus on the present moment.

The first exercise we can practice is mindful breathing. Find a quiet, comfortable place where you can sit or lie down without being disturbed. Start focusing on your breathing, observing the air going in and out of your body. Notice how your chest expands and contracts, how air enters and leaves your nose. If your mind wanders, simply bring your attention back to your breathing. Keep doing this for a few minutes until you feel more relaxed and focused.

Another mindfulness exercise is sense awareness. Try to get in touch with your five senses: sight, hearing, taste, smell and touch. Focus on what you see around you, the sounds you hear, the taste of the food you eat, the smell of flowers or nature, and the feel of the fabric on your clothes or the wind on your skin. This exercise will help you develop greater focus on the present and clear your mind of negative thoughts.

Another mindfulness exercise you can try is the practice of "body scan." This is a practice of being aware of the physical sensations in your body, from the bottom up. Start by focusing your attention on your feet, noticing how your socks or shoes feel. Then, move your attention slowly upward, noticing the sensations in your calves, knees, thighs, and so on, until you reach your head. This exercise will help you develop greater awareness of your body and physical sensations, clearing your mind of negative thoughts.

Finally, the exercise of "metta" or "loving kindness" can help clear the mind of negative thoughts and develop feelings of love and kindness toward oneself and others. Start by imagining a person you love, and mentally repeat, "May this person be happy, may this person be healthy, may this person be safe, may this person have peace." Repeat these phrases for several minutes, focusing on the feelings of love and kindness you have for this person. Then, repeat the same phrases for yourself, imagining that you are sending love and kindness to yourself.

Chapter 7.
Meditation Exercises
to Stop Compulsive Thoughts

Meditation is an ancient practice that has been used for centuries to calm the mind, reduce stress, and develop mind-and-body awareness. Despite its spiritual origin, meditation is a practice that can be adopted by anyone, regardless of their religious or spiritual beliefs. In fact, in recent years, meditation has become increasingly popular as an effective technique for improving mental and physical well-being.

Meditation can take many different forms, but it involves concentration on a specific object or idea, such as the breath or a word or phrase. During meditation, you try to clear your mind of everyday thoughts and worries and enter a state of tranquility and inner peace. In this way, meditation can help reduce stress, anxiety and muscle tension, improving mental and physical health.

Studies have shown that meditation can have numerous mental and physical health benefits. For example, it can help reduce symptoms of depression, anxiety and post-traumatic stress. Meditation can also improve sleep quality, reduce blood pressure and increase the immune system's ability to fight infection.

In addition, meditation can help develop mind and body awareness, which can be helpful in dealing with negative physical sensations and difficult emotions. In fact, through meditation one learns to notice physical sensations and emotions without judging or reacting to them, but simply observing and accepting them. This awareness can help reduce the emotional impact of difficult situations and better manage daily stress.

In summary, meditation can offer numerous mental and physical health benefits. Meditation requires no special equipment or environment, just a little time and commitment. With consistent practice, meditation can help calm the mind, reduce stress, and develop mind-and-body awareness.

Meditation Exercises to Calm Your Mind

There are many meditation techniques available to calm the mind and reduce stress. Some of the most common techniques include breathing meditation, walking meditation, mind void meditation and guided meditation.

Breathing meditation is a very simple exercise involving concentration on breathing. To practice it, simply sit in a quiet place and focus on your breathing so that you notice each inhalation and exhalation. As you pay attention to your breathing, distracting thoughts will begin to fade away, making way for a quieter, more focused mind.

Walking meditation involves concentrating on the movement of the body while walking. It can be practiced anywhere, including outdoors, and involves walking slowly, focusing on body movements, such as the movement of the feet, legs and arms. This technique can help calm the mind and reduce anxiety and stress.

Mental emptiness meditation involves reaching a state of mental tranquility, in which one tries to eliminate all distracting thoughts and worries. To achieve this state, one can focus on an object or sound, such as a burning candle or relaxing music. Over time, the exercise helps achieve a state of mental calm, which can help reduce stress and anxiety.

Guided meditation is an additional technique that involves using an audio recording or instructor to guide the meditation. The instructor provides guidance on body postures, breathing and mental concentration, helping to relax and enter a state of mental calm.

It is important to note that the effectiveness of meditation depends on regularity of practice. To obtain the benefits of meditation, it is necessary to devote time each day to the practice and have the patience to wait for the results to manifest.

Meditation Exercises to Develop Body Awareness

Meditation is a practice to calm the mind and develop awareness of your own body. Many meditation exercises focus on developing awareness of your breathing, physical sensations, emotions, and thoughts, as well as how they manifest in your body.

An example of a meditation exercise to develop body awareness is body scan meditation. This technique involves lying down on a mat or bed and focusing on the sensation of each part of the body, starting from the head and reaching down to the feet. During the body scan, one can notice physical sensations such as muscle tension, heat, cold, or tingling sensation. The goal is to become aware of these sensations without judging them or trying to change them, but simply observing and accepting them.

Another meditation technique for developing body awareness is sense meditation. This technique involves sitting or lying down and focusing on the five senses: sight, hearing, smell, taste and touch. You can start by noticing the sounds around you, then focus on the scents in the air, then the tastes in your mouth, then the feel of the fabric on your skin, and finally the sight of your surroundings. The goal is to become aware of sensations in more detail and to focus on the sensory experience in the present moment.

In general, meditation is a practice that requires perseverance and dedication, but even just a few minutes a day can make a big difference. Regularly practicing meditation exercises to develop body awareness can help reduce stress, improve physical and mental well-being, and increase the ability to be mindful of the present.

An example of body scan meditation is as follows:

1. Find a quiet place to sit or lie down comfortably.

2. Close your eyes and breathe deeply for a few minutes, while focusing your attention on your breathing.

3. Begin to scan your body mentally from your toes to your head, while trying to feel every body part individually.

4. When you get to a body part that feels tense or sore, stop scanning and focus your attention on that area instead.

5. Breathe in deeply, while imagining that you are sending fresh, clean air directly to the area of the body where you feel tension or pain.

6. Exhale slowly, while imagining that you are expelling the tension from the affected area, along with your breath.

7. Keep breathing in and out this way, while focusing on the physical sensations in your body and letting go of tension with each exhale.

8. When you are ready, resume the body scan and continue until you have explored every body part.

This body scan meditation exercise helps develop awareness of the body and physical sensations, reducing tension and stress in the body.

Meditation Exercises to Manage Physical Pain and Anxiety

Meditation exercises can be useful not only to calm the mind and develop awareness, but also to manage negative physical sensations such as pain or physical anxiety. In this section, we will explore some meditation exercises that can help manage these feelings and improve physical well-being.

One of the most common techniques for dealing with negative physical feelings is diaphragmatic breath meditation. This technique involves focusing on the inhalation and exhalation of breath, bringing attention to the diaphragm and chest movement during breathing. The goal is to breathe smoothly and deeply, creating a relaxed and calm state. This technique can be helpful in reducing muscle pain and physical anxiety.

Another useful meditation exercise to deal with negative physical feelings is mantra meditation. In this technique, you will choose a mantra (e.g., a word) that has personal meaning, and you will repeat this mantra mentally during meditation. This mantra will help you focus your positive energy on reducing stress and anxiety. This technique can also help reduce physical pain, as it gives you something else to focus on.

In addition, physical sensation meditation is another useful exercise for dealing with negative physical sensations. In this technique, you focus your attention on a specific body part or physical sensation, such as pain or tingling. The goal is to observe the sensation without judging it or trying to change it. This technique helps develop awareness of the body and physical sensations, improving the management of physical pain and anxiety.

In summary, there are several meditation techniques that can be used to manage negative physical sensations. Diaphragmatic breath meditation, mantra meditation, and physical sensation meditation are just some of the techniques that can be used to achieve greater physical and mental well-being. Try exploring these techniques and finding the one that works best for you.

How to Integrate Meditation into Your Daily Life

Integrating meditation into your daily life can seem challenging—especially if you are always busy. However, there are many strategies that can help you find the time to practice meditation during the day. One of the simplest techniques is to find just a few minutes during the day to meditate (e.g., a five-minute meditation break during work, before starting a new task, or after a coffee break).

In addition, one can meditate during the home-to-work or home-to-school commute. One can take a few minutes to sit comfortably in the car or on public transportation and practice a short meditation on breathing or body awareness. Even during lunch breaks or while moving from one room to another, you can take a few minutes to close your eyes and focus on your breathing.

Some people find it useful to create a space dedicated to meditation in their home or office. One can choose a quiet corner of the home or office and decorate it with a few items that promote relaxation, such as scented candles or plants. In this way, you will have a space where you can meditate when you need a break.

Finally, one can also meditate during daily activities such as cleaning the house or preparing food. For example, during house cleaning one can focus on the sensation of cleaning the floors or the sound of vacuuming. During food preparation, on the other hand, one can focus on the sensation of handling food or the smell of ingredients.

In general, the important thing is to find the time and space to meditate throughout the day, even if only for a few minutes. Integrating meditation into daily life can help reduce stress, anxiety and maintain a greater awareness of the present moment.

How to Overcome Difficulties During Meditation Practice

Meditation practice can be difficult for many people, especially those who are new to meditation. However, there are some common difficulties that can be overcome with a little patience and perseverance.

One of the most common difficulties is the difficulty in concentrating. When trying to meditate, the mind can easily digress and focus on external thoughts, worries and distractions. In this case, a useful technique is to focus on breathing. One can count the breaths or focus on the movement of the breath as it goes in and out of the body. Alternatively, one can use a mantra or a repetitive phrase to keep the mind focused.

Another common difficulty is anxiety. When trying to meditate, anxiety can increase and interfere with the ability to relax and concentrate. In this case, you can use deep breathing techniques to calm the mind and body. You can inhale slowly through your nose, hold your breath for a few seconds, and then exhale slowly through your mouth. This technique helps to reduce anxiety and promote inner calm.

Frustration is another common difficulty in meditation practice. When you are unable to meditate as you wish, you may feel frustrated and discouraged. In this case, it is important to remember that meditation practice takes time and perseverance. One can start with a few minutes a day and gradually increase the time of meditation. In addition, one can seek support from meditation groups or qualified teachers to help overcome frustration and maintain motivation.

In summary, practicing meditation may involve some difficulties, but these can be overcome with specific techniques such as focusing on breathing, deep breathing, and gradually increasing the meditation time. In addition, the support of meditation groups or qualified teachers can be very helpful in overcoming difficulties and maintaining motivation.

Chapter 8.
Breathing Exercises
to Relax and Reduce Stress

Breathing is a vital process that allows us to absorb oxygen from the air and expel carbon dioxide, but it can also be used as a tool to manage stress and anxiety. When we are stressed or anxious, our bodies tend to breathe quickly and shallowly, which can increase the level of cortisol in the blood, a hormone associated with the stress response.

However, mindful breathing can help reverse this stress response. When we focus on making our breathing deeper and slower, we can calm the mind and relax the body, thereby reducing cortisol levels in the blood. In addition, breathing can affect the autonomic nervous system, which controls involuntary bodily functions (e.g., heart rate and digestion). When we breathe deeply and slowly, we can activate the parasympathetic nervous system, which relaxes and repairs the body.

In addition, there are some breathing techniques that can have specific effects on the body and mind. For example, diaphragmatic breathing, which involves breathing through the diaphragm instead of the chest, can increase the amount of oxygen reaching the lungs and reduce muscle tension, improving relaxation. Yogic breathing, which involves breathing through only one nostril at a time, can also be used to balance the nervous system and increase self-awareness.

In summary, mindful breathing is an important stress management technique that can help reduce muscle tension, calm the mind, and relax the body, thereby improving overall health and well-being. Breathing techniques can be used anytime, anywhere and require no special equipment or preparation, making them a simple yet effective tool for stress and anxiety management.

Breathing Techniques for Relaxation

There are many breathing techniques that can help achieve a state of relaxation and tranquility. Among the most common breathing techniques for relaxation are diaphragmatic breathing, deep breathing, and yogic breathing.

Diaphragmatic breathing is a deep-breathing technique that involves the diaphragm, which is the muscle found underneath the lungs. The diaphragm helps expand the lungs during breathing. To perform diaphragmatic breathing, first lie down or sit in a comfortable position, then place one hand on your chest, and the other on your stomach. Inhale slowly through your nose, while feeling the air entering your stomach and pushing your hand outward. Exhale slowly through your mouth, while feeling your stomach contracting, and your hand moving inward. This type of breathing helps relax your neck and shoulder muscles, reduce muscle tension, and increase the oxygen in your blood.

Deep breathing is another breathing technique that can help reduce stress and anxiety. To perform deep breathing, you should start by sitting or standing with your back straight and your hands on your knees. Breathe in slowly through the nose, pushing air down into the belly and causing the abdomen to expand. Exhale slowly through the mouth, feeling the belly contract and the air being expelled. This type of breathing helps improve body awareness, reduce muscle tension and calm the mind.

Yogic breathing is a breathing technique used in yoga that involves alternating between the nostrils to balance the nervous system. To perform yogic breathing, you should start by sitting with your back straight and your hands resting on your knees.

Inhale through one nostril, covering the other with your thumb. Exhale through the other nostril, covering the other with the ring finger. Continue breathing in this way, alternating nostrils with each breath. This type of breathing helps balance the nervous system and improve awareness of the body and mind.

In conclusion, there are many breathing techniques that can help achieve a state of relaxation and tranquility. Diaphragmatic breathing, deep breathing and yogic breathing are just some of the breathing techniques that can be used to reduce muscle tension, improve oxygenation of the body and calm the mind. Experimenting with different breathing techniques and finding the one that works best for you can help you manage stress and anxiety effectively.

How to Practice Breathing Exercises

To practice breathing exercises effectively, it is important to find a quiet and comfortable place where you can relax. It is important to find a place where you feel comfortable and where there are as few distractions as possible. For some people, this might be a quiet, peaceful room, while for others it might be a park or a beach.

Once you have found a suitable place, it is important to sit comfortably and adopt a relaxed, upright posture. You may choose to sit cross-legged or in a chair, while making sure you have good posture. Your chin should be slightly retracted, and your shoulders should be relaxed, with no stiffness.

Once you are sitting comfortably, you can begin to focus on breathing. You may choose to close your eyes or stare at a point in front of you. Begin by slowly inhaling through your nose, bringing air into your belly and expanding your diaphragm. Hold the air in your lungs for a few seconds and then exhale slowly through your mouth.

For diaphragmatic breathing, it is important to focus on the sensation of air entering and leaving the body. Inhale deeply through the nose, expanding the diaphragm and causing the abdomen to inflate. Exhale slowly through the mouth, causing the diaphragm to deflate and retract the abdomen.

In yogic breathing, or pranayama, the focus is on breathing through the nostrils. By inhaling through one nostril and then exhaling through the other, the flow of energy through the body can be regulated.

Finally, deep breathing involves full use of the lungs. Begin by inhaling slowly through the nose, causing the chest and diaphragm to expand. Hold the air in the lungs for a few seconds and then exhale slowly through the mouth, causing the diaphragm and chest to contract.

In summary, to practice breathing exercises effectively, it is important to find a quiet and comfortable place, adopt a relaxed but upright posture, focus on breathing, and use techniques such as diaphragmatic breathing, yogic breathing, and deep breathing.

Examples of Breathing Exercises

There are many breathing techniques used in meditative practice.

Here are some of them:

• **Diaphragmatic Breathing:** This technique involves inhaling through your nose so that your diaphragm inflates, then exhaling through your mouth. Your breath should be slow and deep, thus allowing air to flow in and out in a natural, relaxed way.

• **Alternating Breathing:** This technique involves inhaling through one nostril and exhaling through the other. Alternate between nostrils with each breath, thus creating an alternating airflow through both nostrils.

• **Square Breathing:** This technique involves inhaling while mentally counting to four, then holding your breath for another four seconds, followed by exhaling for four seconds, and finally holding your breath at the end of the exhale for another four seconds. Then repeat.

• **4-7-8 Breathing:** This technique involves inhaling through your nose for four seconds, then holding your breath for seven seconds, and finally exhaling through your mouth for eight seconds.

• **Deep Breathing:** This technique involves breathing deeply through your nose, thus causing your chest and diaphragm to inflate, then exhaling slowly through your mouth and deflating your chest and diaphragm.

Each of these techniques can be used to calm the mind and rid it of negative thoughts during meditation.

Diaphragmatic Breathing

Diaphragmatic breathing, also called abdominal breathing or deep breathing, is a breathing technique that involves using the diaphragm to breathe instead of the shoulder and chest muscles. The diaphragm is a dome-shaped muscle that separates the chest from the abdomen and contracts and relaxes to allow air to enter and exit the lungs.

To perform diaphragmatic breathing correctly, one should sit comfortably in a quiet place and focus on breathing.

You should then place one hand on your abdomen and the other on your chest. Begin to inhale slowly through the nose, causing the abdomen to expand like a balloon. The hand placed on the chest should not move. Then, exhale slowly through the mouth, feeling the abdomen relax and move back toward the spine.

Diaphragmatic breathing can help reduce stress and anxiety as it causes the body to relax and restore the normal balance of oxygen and carbon dioxide. It is also helpful in improving posture, increasing lung capacity and reducing muscle tension.

This technique can be used as a part of meditative practice or as a daily breathing exercise. It can also be combined with other relaxation techniques (e.g., guided visualization or body awareness).

Alternate Breathing

Alternate breathing, also known as Nadi Shodhana in Sanskrit, is a breathing technique that is often used in yoga practice and meditation. This breathing technique involves using both nostrils alternately to help calm the mind and balance the nervous system.

To begin, you assume a comfortable sitting position with a straight back. You cover your right thumb with your ring finger and pinky finger, leaving your index and middle fingers free. With the middle finger, you gently press on the right nostril to close it, then slowly inhale through the left nostril. When you reach the end of the inhalation, you close the left nostril with your index finger and slowly exhale through the right nostril. Then you inhale through the right nostril, close it with your little finger and exhale through the left nostril. This breathing cycle is repeated for several minutes, alternating nostrils.

Alternate breathing is useful for calming the mind and relaxing the body, but it is also known to improve concentration and memory. In addition, this technique can help reduce stress and anxiety, improve sleep quality and lower blood pressure.

Square Breathing

Square breathing (also known as "pranayama" in yoga practice) is a breathing technique that involves controlling your breath using a regular, steady rhythm. This technique is called "square" breathing because each phase (i.e., inhalation, first pause, exhalation, and second pause) is performed for the same amount of time, thus creating an imaginary 4x4 square.

To perform square breathing, you need to sit in a comfortable position, keep your spine straight and focus on breathing.

The technique consists of following the following steps:

1. Breathe slowly, while mentally counting to four.
2. Hold your breath, while mentally counting to four.
3. Exhale slowly, while mentally counting to four.
4. Hold your breath again, while mentally counting to four.

The process can be repeated several times, gradually increasing the number of cycles according to personal needs.

Square breathing is a very useful technique for calming the mind and relaxing the body, as it regulates the heart rate and promotes concentration. It is particularly effective during times of anxiety, stress or nervousness, but can also be practiced during meditation or exercise to improve breathing and increase body awareness.

The 4-7-8 Breathing Technique

This technique is a breathing technique that uses a specific breathing rhythm to calm the mind and reduce stress and anxiety.

Here is how to perform this technique:
1. Breathe slowly through your nose, while counting to four.
2. Hold your breath for seven seconds.
3. Exhale slowly through your mouth, while counting to eight.

This complete cycle should last about 15 seconds.

The 4-7-8 breathing technique is often used as a part of meditation practice or to calm the mind before falling asleep. Slow, controlled breathing helps reduce your heart rate and lower your blood pressure by stimulating the parasympathetic nervous system, which calms your body and mind.

This technique can be performed anytime, anywhere, as it does not require any special tools or instruments. It is important to perform it in a quiet environment without distractions to focus on breathing and experience its beneficial effects.

Deep Breathing

Deep breathing (also known as "abdominal breathing" or "diaphragmatic breathing") is a breathing technique that involves the diaphragm, which is a muscle found under the lungs. The diaphragm helps regulate the breathing process.

To practice deep breathing, it is important to sit in a comfortable position and keep your back straight. You can place one hand on your chest and the other on your stomach to help you focus on abdominal breathing.

To begin, you inhale slowly through the nose, making sure that the air fills the diaphragm first and then the lungs. You may notice that the abdomen swells slightly during inhalation. Once you reach maximum inhalation, you hold your breath for a few seconds, then slowly exhale through your mouth, trying to empty your lungs completely.

It is important to focus on abdominal breathing, rather than chest breathing, to get the maximum benefits from deep breathing. Deep breathing can help reduce stress and anxiety, improve blood circulation, and increase blood oxygenation.

Deep breathing can be used at any time of the day, even when sitting at work or during a break. You can also combine deep breathing with other meditation techniques to enhance your practice.

Integrating Breathing into Your Daily Life

Breathing is a bodily function that we often take for granted, but it can be used strategically to improve our overall well-being and reduce stress in our daily lives. Integrating breathing into your daily life may seem difficult, but it is easy if you follow a few tips.

One of the first things one can do is to take breaks during work to focus on breathing. This can be done at any time, even for just a few seconds, by taking a few deep breaths and focusing on the flow of air in and out of our bodies. This can help us relax and focus better on the tasks we are doing, improving productivity.

Breathing can also be integrated into your daily life during your commute. This can be done simply by focusing on breathing while driving or by using specific breathing techniques, such as diaphragmatic breathing, which involves the diaphragm. The diaphragm is a muscle found underneath the lungs that can help reduce stress and anxiety.

You can also integrate breathing into your daily activities (e.g., cleaning and cooking). For example, while sweeping or preparing lunch, you can pay attention to your breathing by focusing on inhaling, exhaling, and coordinating your breath with your body movements. This can help reduce stress and muscle tension.

There are also specific breathing techniques that can be performed quickly and easily at any time of the day. For example, the 4-7-8 breathing technique involves inhaling for 4 seconds, holding the breath for 7 seconds and then exhaling slowly for 8 seconds. This type of breathing can help reduce stress and anxiety in a matter of minutes.

Ultimately, integrating breathing into daily life can be an excellent strategy for improving overall well-being and reducing stress. There are many different ways to do this, from breaks during work to specific breathing techniques, and everyone can find the one that works best for them.

Chapter 9.
Visualization Exercises
to Create a Positive Mindset

Visualization is a relaxation and mind-strengthening technique that involves using one's imagination to create positive images and situations in one's mind. Visualization is an ancient practice, dating back to ancient cultures such as ancient Greece, where athletes used visualization to prepare for competitions.

Visualization can be used for a wide range of purposes, including achieving personal goals, managing stress, increasing motivation, reducing anxiety and pain, and creating a state of general well-being.

To use visualization effectively, it is important to have a clear and specific goal in mind. For example, if the goal is to improve one's health, visualization could be used to imagine one's body in a perfect state of health and well-being. Similarly, if the goal is to achieve some success in one's professional life, visualization could be used to imagine oneself in a position of success and job satisfaction.

Visualization works by stimulating mental processes—particularly, those involving perception, memory, and imagination. When visualizing, your mind creates images that come as close as possible to reality, thus stimulating the same brainwaves that are activated when you actually experience what you are imagining.

The use of visualization requires a certain degree of skill and practice, but with training, one can develop the ability to visualize in detail and vividly. In addition, there are many variations of visualization to suit different personality types and individual preferences.

In summary, visualization is an effective technique for improving one's psychological and physical well-being. Using one's imagination, one can create positive images and situations in one's mind, which help to achieve desired goals and overcome obstacles. With practice, visualization can become an integral part of one's daily routine, helping to create a positive, goal-focused mind.

Benefits of Visualization

The benefits of visualization are many and varied. In this technique, the mind creates vivid and realistic images to achieve goals, and this leads to a positive effect on mental and physical health. Let's see what the main benefits of visualization are.

One of the first benefits of visualization is stress reduction. Regular practice of visualization can help relax the mind and body, reducing muscle tension and decreasing anxiety levels. This is an effective way to deal with the discomfort and nervousness often caused by daily stress.

Visualization helps you focus on your goals by visualizing the result and imagining all the steps needed to achieve it. Visualization can improve your concentration and increase your motivation and determination to pursue your set goals.

Visualization can also help in managing emotions. The vivid images created in the mind during visualization can help you better recognize, understand and manage your emotions. Visualization can be used to cope with emotionally difficult situations, to prepare for stressful situations, or to increase emotional awareness.

Finally, visualization can help achieve goals with greater ease. Visualizing an achieved goal and imagining all the steps needed to reach it can increase the likelihood of success. Visualization can also help identify any obstacles along the way and find solutions to overcome them.

To recap, visualization is an effective technique for creating a positive, goal-focused mind. Regular practice of visualization can bring many benefits, including stress reduction, increased concentration and motivation, better management of emotions, and ease in achieving goals.

How to Prepare for Visualization

To get the maximum benefit from visualization, it is important to prepare properly. Preparation involves creating a suitable environment, choosing the most comfortable position and deep breathing.

First, it is important to find a quiet and peaceful place where you can perform the visualization without distraction. In this way, you can focus more on your goals and the visualization itself, without being disturbed by outside noise or interruptions.

Second, the position you are in during the visualization is very important. Choosing a comfortable position, such as sitting on a chair or pillow, can help you relax and avoid any physical discomfort that might distract from the visualization. Also, keeping your back straight and shoulders relaxed during the visualization helps to maintain focus and concentration.

Finally, deep breathing is a key element in preparing for visualization. Breathing in deeply and then exhaling slowly helps you relax and focus on the visualization goal. Deep breathing helps to reduce stress and calm the mind, creating an ideal environment for visualization.

Thus, preparation is an essential part of the visualization process. Preparing properly by creating a peaceful and quiet environment, choosing a comfortable position and practicing deep breathing helps create the ideal conditions for visualization. With proper preparation, you can increase the effectiveness of visualization and achieve your goals with greater ease.

Visualization Exercises to Achieve Your Goals

Visualization is a powerful technique for achieving one's goals. There are many visualization exercises that can be used to help manifest what you want in your life.

The following are four examples of visualization exercises that can help you achieve your goals:

1. Imagine a Future Event: This can be anything from a job interview to a romantic encounter. The goal is to imagine the event as you want it to happen by visualizing every detail. You can imagine the emotions you will feel, the actions you will take, and the things you will say. This exercise can help you create confidence and prepare for the event in question.

2. Imagine Your Ideal Life: This exercise requires you to imagine the life you want, from the perfect house to the ideal job. You can imagine the people you want in your life, and the activities you want to do. The goal of this exercise is to help you create a clear vision of your ideal future and focus on what you really want.

3. Visualize the Solution to a Problem: This exercise requires you to imagine the problem as it currently stands, and then imagine the ideal solution. Imagine the actions you will take to solve the problem, and the positive emotions you will feel once the problem is solved. This exercise can help you find creative solutions to problems and maintain a positive attitude.

4. Imagine Achieving Your Goals: This exercise requires you to imagine the results you want to achieve and visualize them as if you have already done so. You can imagine the positive emotions you will feel when the goal has been achieved, and the actions you will take to get the result. This exercise can help you maintain a positive attitude and focus on your goals.

These are just a few examples of visualization exercises that can help you achieve your goals. Remember that visualization is a personal practice, and you can customize it to suit your needs and preferences. There are many visualization exercises that can be used to help manifest what you want in your life. The key to success is constant practice and focus on visualizing your desired goals.

How to Make Visualization More Effective

To make visualization more effective, there are some useful tips that can be followed. One of these is to visualize with all the senses. When visualizing a goal or outcome, it is important not only to imagine the scene visually, but also to involve the other senses such as smell, taste, touch, and hearing. For example, if you are visualizing a trip to a beautiful beach, you might imagine the sound of the waves, the smell of the saltiness, the warmth of the sun on your skin, the taste of the local food, etc.

Another tip for making visualization more effective is to focus on specific details. When visualizing, it is important to focus on the most important details of the image or scene. For example, if you visualize an ideal house, it is important to visualize the details of the house, such as the color of the walls, the type of furniture, the arrangement of objects, etc.

In addition, to make visualization more effective, it is important to visualize with emotion. When visualizing a goal or achievement, it is important to feel the positive emotions associated with that achievement. For example, if you visualize a professional goal, it is important to feel the emotion of success, satisfaction, and accomplishment.

Other useful tips to make visualization more effective are regularity, patience and constant effort. Visualization takes time and commitment to become effective. It is important to visualize regularly, every day or at least once a week, to get the best results. In addition, it is important to have patience and devote time to the practice of visualization to get the desired results.

These tips can help make visualization more effective and achieve better results. Visualizing with all the senses, focusing on specific details, and visualizing with emotion are just some of the useful techniques for improving visualization. In addition, regularity, patience, and consistent effort are key to getting the best results.

How to Overcome Mental Blocks with Visualization

Mental blocks and negative thoughts are often responsible for failure to achieve goals. However, visualization can help overcome these mental blocks and focus on desired outcomes.

First, visualization can help identify the mental blocks and negative thoughts that prevent the achievement of goals. Once identified, one can use visualization to overcome them. For example, if you have a mental block regarding the fear of failure, you can visualize yourself achieving your desired goal and feel happy and satisfied with your success.

In addition, visualization can help boost your self-esteem, which is a key element of overcoming mental blocks. Visualizing yourself achieving your desired goals can boost your self-confidence and motivate you to achieve more.

Visualization can also help change your perspective on a situation and find creative solutions to problems. If you find yourself in a difficult or complicated situation, then visualizing yourself in the situation and imagining how to solve it can help you produce new ideas and solutions.

Finally, visualization can help you stay focused on your goals and keep your motivation high. Visualizing yourself achieving your desired goals can be an excellent source of inspiration and motivation.

In summary, visualization can help overcome mental blocks and negative thoughts that prevent goal achievement, increase self-confidence and motivation, find creative solutions to problems, and stay focused on the end goal.

Chapter 10.
Movement and Stretching
Exercises to Release Tension

Physical activity is a key component of mental health. Many scientific studies show that regular exercise can improve mood, reduce stress and anxiety, and increase self-esteem and self-confidence.

Physical activity has been shown to benefit mental health, as movement helps reduce stress levels and improve mood. Exercise increases the endorphin production. Endorphins are chemicals produced in the body. They function as natural analgesics that help reduce pain and improve mood.

In addition, physical activity can help reduce symptoms of anxiety and depression. A 2018 study published in the journal BMC Public Health showed that exercise can reduce symptoms of anxiety and depression, improve mood and self-esteem, and increase overall sense of well-being.

Physical activity can also help prevent the development of mental health problems. A 2019 study published in the journal Lancet Psychiatry showed that regular physical activity can prevent the development of mental health problems, such as depression and anxiety, in people with a high risk of developing such problems.

Finally, exercise can also increase self-esteem and self-confidence. Physical activity can help improve physical appearance, increase physical strength and stamina, and improve self-image. In addition, physical activity can help develop the ability to concentrate and control emotions, improving the ability to cope with difficult situations.

In summary, regular physical activity is essential for mental and physical health. Exercise can improve mood, reduce stress and anxiety, increase self-esteem and self-confidence, and prevent the development of mental health problems.

Stretching Exercises
to Reduce Muscular Tension

Stretching is a very important technique for reducing muscle tension and improving the health of our body. The term stretching refers to a series of exercises that stretch muscles, improve the elasticity of muscle tissue, prevent injury, and reduce muscle tension. The advantage of stretching is that it can be done anywhere, anytime, without the need for special equipment or moving to a gym. In addition, stretching exercises can be adapted to individual needs and abilities, making it a suitable activity for all ages and fitness levels.

There are several stretching exercises that can be done to reduce muscle tension in different parts of the body. For example, for the shoulders, one can do exercises such as shoulder rotation, arm extension up, and arm rotation. For the neck, on the other hand, one can do exercises such as lateral neck flexion, neck rotation, and head tilt. For the back, on the other hand, one can do exercises such as forward bending, back twisting, and bridging. For the legs, one can do exercises such as knee flexion, hip rotation, and leg flexion. Finally, for the arms, one can do exercises such as wrist flexion, wrist rotation, and forearm flexion.

It is important to note that when stretching, you should take care not to force the muscles too hard. Stretching exercises should always be done slowly to avoid sudden and abrupt movements that could cause injury. In addition, it is important to breathe deeply during the exercises to relax and improve the effects of the stretch.

So, stretching exercises are a very useful technique for reducing muscle tension and improving the health of our body. Due to their simplicity and flexibility, they can be done anywhere and anytime, adapting them to individual needs and abilities. However, it is important to be careful and not force the muscles too much, thus avoiding the risk of injury.

Here are some examples of stretching exercises for different parts of the body:

• **Shoulder Stretch:** Lift your shoulders toward your ears and hold the position for 5-10 seconds, then relax. Repeat five times.

• **Neck Stretch:** Bow your head toward your chest and hold the position for 5-10 seconds, then return to an upright position. Tilt your head to the right, while keeping your left shoulder low, and hold the position for 5-10 seconds. Return to center, then repeat to the left. Finally, tilt your head back, look toward the ceiling, and hold the position for 5-10 seconds.

• **Back Stretch:** Sit on the floor with your legs outstretched. Slowly bend your torso forward, while trying to reach your toes with your fingertips. Hold the position for 10-15 seconds. Repeat 3-5 times.

• **Leg Stretch:** While standing, lift your foot off the floor, bend your right knee, and grab your ankle with your right hand. Bring your heel toward your butt and hold the position for 10-15 seconds. Repeat with your left leg.

• **Arm Stretch:** While standing, extend your right arm in front of you and bend your elbow toward your chest. Grasp your elbow with your left hand and gently push your right arm toward your chest. Hold the position for 10-15 seconds and repeat with your left arm.

These exercises can be customized according to one's needs and flexibility. In addition, it is important to perform the exercises correctly and without forcing the muscles too hard to avoid injury.

Yoga for Mental Health

Yoga is a form of exercise and meditation that has been practiced for centuries for the health of the body and mind. Many experts agree that yoga can be an excellent activity to reduce stress, anxiety and mental tension. In this section, we will explore yoga exercises that can help improve mental health.

Child's pose, also known as Balasana, is a relaxation pose that can help reduce tension in the lower back, shoulders and neck. To perform this pose, you start on your knees with your feet together and your knees spread as wide as your hips. You bend your torso forward, trying to touch the floor with your forehead; your arms can be stretched forward or relaxed at the sides of your body.

Warrior's pose, or Virabhadrasana, is a series of three postures that can help improve the stability and strength of the legs and back while reducing muscle tension. To perform this posture, start in a standing position, bring one foot forward and bend the knee to 90 degrees, keeping the back foot planted on the ground. The arms can be extended upward or forward as you hold the position for a few breaths, then switch sides.

Tree pose, or Vrksasana, is a balancing pose that can help improve concentration and reduce stress. To perform this posture, one starts in a standing position, lifts one foot and rests the sole of the foot on the thighs of the other leg, trying to maintain balance. You bring your hands together in prayer in front of your chest and hold the position for a few breaths, then switch sides.

Cobra pose, or Bhujangasana, is a posture that can help reduce tension in the lower back, improving flexibility of the spine. To perform this pose, you start on the floor, with your hands resting on the floor on either side of your shoulders. You slowly lift your torso off the floor, keeping your legs extended and your feet planted on the floor. You hold the position for a few breaths, then slowly release your torso to the floor.

These are just a few examples of yoga postures that can be used to reduce mental and physical tension. Yoga is a highly customizable activity and can be adapted to individual needs. It is advisable to seek out a qualified yoga instructor to learn the correct postures and achieve maximum mental and physical health benefits.

Physical Exercises to Relieve Stress

Physical activity is an important ally for mental health.
One of the most common exercises that can be done to reduce emotional tension is running. Running is a form of aerobic exercise that engages the whole body and can help release tension built up in the muscles. In addition, running can be a social activity that can be done with friends or in a group, thus also increasing the social dimension of mental well-being.

Dance is another form of exercise that can help reduce emotional tension and improve mood. Dance engages the entire body, allowing tension to be released and flexibility to be improved. In addition, dance can be a form of creative expression that helps develop self-awareness and self-esteem.

Cardio training is another form of exercise that can help reduce emotional tension and improve mood. Cardio workout engages the whole body, increasing blood circulation and improving cardiovascular health. In addition, cardio workout can help release stored energy, improve mood and motivation.

In addition, many other forms of physical activity can be used to improve mental health and reduce stress. Yoga, for example, is a form of physical activity that can help reduce stress and mental tension by improving flexibility and concentration. Walking can also be a useful form of exercise for mental health, helping to reduce emotional tension and improve sleep quality.

In general, any form of physical activity can be helpful in reducing emotional tension and improving mental health. The important thing is to find a physical activity that fits your lifestyle and interests so that it becomes a regular and enjoyable part of your daily routine.

The Importance of Rest and Sleep for Mental Health

Rest and sleep are essential for mental and physical health. Sleep helps restore and repair the body and mind after a long day, providing time to consolidate memories, increase concentration and alertness, and reduce stress. However, many people do not get enough or enough sleep, which can negatively affect mental health.

There are several ways to improve sleep quality and promote rest. First, avoid caffeine and other stimulants such as alcohol before sleep. Although these may seem helpful for relaxation, they can interfere with sleep and cause insomnia.

In addition, it is important to create a quiet and comfortable sleeping environment by maintaining a proper temperature, reducing noise and light, and using a comfortable mattress and pillow. Stimulating activities (e.g., watching television or using the phone) should be avoided before you go to bed, as they can interfere with your sleep.

Maintaining a regular sleep-wake rhythm is also important for mental health. This means going to bed and waking up at the same time every day, even on weekends. This trains the body to recognize when it is time to sleep and when it is time to be awake, improving sleep quality and overall mental health.

In summary, rest and sleep are critical for mental and physical health. To improve sleep quality, it is important to avoid caffeine and other stimulants, create a quiet and comfortable sleeping environment, and maintain a regular sleep-wake rhythm. In this way, you can reduce stress and improve mental health.

Chapter 11.
How to Set Realistic Goals
to Improve Your Mental Health

Setting realistic and attainable goals is crucial for psychological well-being and the reduction of stress and anxiety. Often, people feel overwhelmed by their goals, especially if they are unrealistic or too ambitious, and this can lead to a sense of failure, frustration, and stress.

When you set a realistic goal, on the other hand, you are more likely to achieve it, and this in turn can improve your self-esteem and sense of accomplishment. In addition, the experience of achieving a goal can have a positive impact on mental health, increasing motivation and self-confidence.

Setting realistic goals also means understanding your capabilities and resources. It is important to consider the time, knowledge, skills, and financial resources needed to achieve your set goal so that you will not feel overwhelmed or unmotivated and so that you can decide which steps you will need to take to achieve your goal.

However, setting realistic goals does not mean giving up on your dreams or not challenging yourself. On the contrary, it is important to set goals that are ambitious but also reasonable and possible. This involves considering the balance between your personal and professional goals, as well as other factors (e.g., your family life, work responsibilities, and activities that you do in your spare time).

So, setting realistic and achievable goals is an important tool for preventing stress and anxiety, maintaining good mental health, and achieving success in a healthy and sustainable way. This requires a realistic assessment of one's capabilities and resources, as well as an understanding of one's personal and professional priorities.

Find Your Goals

To achieve the goals we set for ourselves, it is essential to know exactly what we want to achieve and how we can do it. Identifying one's goals, therefore, is the crucial first step in achieving them.

First, determine the goals you wish to achieve. Choose both short-term and long-term goals. Short-term goals are those that can be achieved in a short period of time (e.g., a week or month). Long-term goals take a longer period (e.g., 5-10 years).

Once your goals have been identified, it is important to assess their feasibility and understand whether the goals you have chosen are realistic, and whether you can achieve them.

In this regard, it may be helpful to ask ourselves some questions:

1. "Are the goals I set for myself realistic?"
2. "What should I do to achieve these goals?"
3. "Do I have the resources and skills to achieve these goals?"
4. "What obstacles might stop me from achieving these goals, and how can I overcome them?"

These questions can help us understand whether the goals we have chosen are attainable and what we can do to achieve them.

In addition, it is important to set goals clearly and specifically. For example, if the goal is to "be fitter," this may be too general. Instead, a more specific goal could be "lose 5 kg in 3 months and start exercising regularly." This way, it is easier to understand what we need to do to achieve the goal and how to evaluate our progress.

Thus, identifying one's goals and assessing their feasibility are key steps in setting realistic and achievable goals. Once we have set goals, it is important to make them specific and define an action plan to achieve them.

Choosing the Right Goals

Choosing the right goals is a crucial step in setting realistic and achievable goals. Before deciding which goals are right for us, we need to understand what is important to us and what we want to achieve.

To choose the right goals, it is important to assess our current situation and capabilities, and to consider how much time and effort we are willing to devote to achieving those goals. It is important to be honest with ourselves and not set goals that are too difficult or too easy to achieve.

In addition, we should choose goals based on our priorities and interests. If what we want to achieve is not important to us, we will be less motivated to work hard to achieve it. On the other hand, if we choose a goal that we are passionate about, we will be more motivated and determined to work to achieve it.

It is also important to be realistic about your resources. You need to consider your finances, time, social support, knowledge, and skills to make sure that the goals you choose are possible to achieve.

Finally, it is important to set goals that are in line with our values. If the goals we choose conflict with our core values, it will be difficult for us to achieve them, and we may feel dissatisfied even if we achieve them.

In summary, it is important to choose realistic, attainable goals. You should consider your current situation, capabilities, resources, interests, priorities, and values to ensure that you set challenging, possible, and meaningful goals.

How to Break Goals into Achievable Steps

One of the main reasons why people do not achieve their goals is because they are too large or complex to tackle at once. The solution is to break the goals down into smaller steps to make them easier to tackle and achieve.

For example, if your goal is to lose 10 pounds, then it may be helpful to break this goal down into smaller steps (e.g., losing one pound at a time, following a healthy eating plan for a month, or exercising regularly). These smaller steps will make the goal more realistic and achievable and will help keep you motivated.

Breaking down the goals into smaller steps is also useful for addressing complex or multi-step goals. For example, if the goal is to learn a new language, you can break it down into steps such as learning the basics of grammar, learning basic vocabulary, practicing reading and writing, and finally improving listening and speaking skills.

Once goals have been broken down into smaller steps, it is important to track your progress so that you can keep track of your successes, and any obstacles that occur along the way. This can be done using a journal or goal-tracking app. Tracking your progress can help maintain your motivation, identify any difficulties, and find solutions to problems.

In addition, breaking down goals into smaller steps can help prevent feeling overwhelmed and maintain motivation in the long term. In fact, long-term goals often require a lot of time and effort and can cause anxiety and stress. But with a well-defined plan and by breaking the goal down into small, achievable steps, you can achieve the goal without feeling overwhelmed or stressed.

In summary, breaking down goals into smaller steps is an effective way to make goals more realistic and achievable, maintain motivation, track progress, and prevent feeling overwhelmed.

The Importance of Monitoring Your Progress

Monitoring one's progress is critical to achieving one's goals and maintaining motivation in the long run. Without continuous evaluation of one's progress, it can be difficult to know whether one is going in the right direction or achieving the desired results.

To check your progress, it is important to establish clear, specific, and measurable success indicators. For example, if your goal is to lose weight, then a success indicator might be the number of pounds you lose each week. If your goal is to complete a work project, then a success indicator might be the number of hours you work each day, or the number of tasks you complete each week.

Once indicators of success have been established, it is important to keep track of them through tools such as a journal, tracking chart or dedicated app. This allows you to visualize your progress over time and get a clear overview of the areas where you are improving and those that still require more effort.

In addition, monitoring your progress can help identify any obstacles or challenges you meet along the way, thus allowing you to make the right course corrections and maintain your motivation. For example, if a success indicator is not met for several consecutive weeks, then it may be time to revise your action plan or seek support from a coach or expert in the field.

Finally, checking your progress can be an opportunity to celebrate your achievements! Acknowledging and celebrating your successes is critical to maintain high motivation and a positive outlook on the future.

How to Manage Failure

Setting realistic goals does not necessarily mean that you will never meet difficulties or failures along the way. Inevitably, there will be times when your goals and expectations are not met. In these cases, it is important to learn how to manage any failures and not get caught up in stress and anxiety.

First, it is important to learn to recognize that failure is a part of learning and personal growth. No one is perfect, and we all make mistakes. The important thing is to recognize that every failure can be an opportunity to gain experience and improve so that you can avoid falling into a defeatist mentality, while you maintain a positive perspective.

Additionally, it is important to avoid excessive guilt in case of failure. There are many reasons a goal may not be achieved, some of which may be beyond your control. Instead of blaming yourself, it is important to identify the causes of failure rationally and try to learn from past experiences.

Furthermore, it is important not to give up completely in the face of failure. Even if a goal is not achieved, there are always other opportunities to try again and improve. Instead of abandoning the goal completely, you can review the strategy and make any changes needed to increase your chances of success.

For example, you may need to add intermediate steps, seek support from friends or colleagues, or extend the deadline.

Finally, it is important to try to maintain a long-term perspective. Momentary failure should not become an excuse to abandon long-term goals. On the contrary, it can be a challenge that can be overcome with time and perseverance. Sometimes it just takes a little time and dedication to achieve your goals.

In summary, handling failures is an important part of the process of setting realistic goals. Learning to recognize one's mistakes, avoiding excessive blame, not giving up completely, and maintaining a long-term perspective are all key factors in overcoming failures and continuing to move toward set goals.

Practical Tips for Setting Realistic Goals

Setting realistic goals is an important step to achieve success in any area of life. However, for some people, it can be difficult to figure out how to get started and maintain enthusiasm. In this section, I will provide some practical tips to help you set realistic, achievable goals.

The first tip is to write down your goals on a piece of paper or electronic document. This can help clarify exactly what you want to achieve and make it more tangible. In addition, writing down goals can also help you set a deadline by which you want to achieve a particular goal, and define intermediate steps for achieving it.

Another tip is to use a journal to check your progress. This can be useful to see how far you have progressed and whether you are on the right track to reach your goal. In addition, a journal can help you identify any obstacles or problems that you may face while working towards your goal.

In addition, it can be helpful to divide the goals into small steps or intermediate goals. This can help make the final goal less intimidating and more easily attainable. In addition, dividing goals into intermediate steps can also provide a sense of satisfaction when each step is achieved.

Another tip is to find a way to make the goal more fun. For example, if the goal is to lose weight, you can find a way to do fun physical activity, such as dancing or going for a walk with a friend. This way, the goal becomes less strenuous and more enjoyable, making it easier to maintain over time.

Finally, it is important not to get caught up in stress or frustration in case of failure. There will always be obstacles and failures along the way, but it is important to learn from these mistakes and keep working toward the goal set. Recognizing that failures are part of the learning process can help you stay motivated and focused on the end goal.

In summary, setting realistic, attainable goals requires some effort and planning, but it can be very rewarding. Using these practical tips, you can start working toward your goals more efficiently and stress-free!

Chapter 12.
Using Gratitude
to Instantly Clear Your Mind

Gratitude is one of the most powerful emotions we can feel. It is a feeling of gratitude and appreciation for what we have in our lives, both big and small. It can be practiced in many forms, from verbal expressions of gratitude to positive thoughts that run through our minds.

The practice of gratitude is important because it helps us focus our attention on what we have rather than on what we lack. Often, we focus on our problems and difficulties in life, but gratitude allows us to look on the bright side and appreciate the little things that make us happy.

There is much research proving the mental and physical health benefits of gratitude. For example, a study conducted by the Greater Good Science Center at the University of California at Berkeley showed that practicing gratitude can increase happiness and reduce depression. Another study showed that gratitude can improve sleep quality and reduce anxiety symptoms.

In addition, gratitude can help improve interpersonal relationships. When we are grateful for what others do for us, we tend to be kinder and more respectful toward them, which can lead to more satisfying and lasting relationships.

Finally, the practice of gratitude can help develop resilience. When we are grateful for what we have in our lives, it becomes easier to cope with difficulties and overcome adversity. Gratitude helps us focus on our strengths and the resources we have available to us, rather than on our weaknesses and the things we lack.

There are many forms of gratitude that can be practiced every day; incorporating them into your daily life can have lasting effects on your health and well-being.

How to Practice Gratitude

There are many different techniques that can be used to practice gratitude, and each of them has its advantages. Below, we will provide some examples of common techniques that can be used to cultivate gratitude in daily life.

One of the most common techniques for practicing gratitude is to keep a gratitude journal. This involves writing down a list of things you are grateful for each day, whether big or small. This practice can help you focus on the positives in life and consider all the good things that happen to us each day. Starting or ending the day with this practice can help develop a good mood and positivity.

Another common technique is to make a list of things for which you are grateful. This can be done on a daily, weekly or monthly basis. It involves listing the things we are grateful for, such as health, family, friends, work, home, nature, and more. This exercise can help you focus on the positives in life and appreciate the things we often take for granted.

Expressing gratitude to someone directly is another powerful technique. This can be done through a text message, a phone call or a face-to-face meeting. Expressing gratitude helps create stronger bonds with others, improves communication and empathy, makes relationships stronger, and increases happiness for both of us. This practice is especially helpful when we feel dissatisfied or unfortunate in life.

Finally, there are many other techniques for practicing gratitude that can be useful in your daily life (e.g., gratitude meditation, setting daily reminders to practice gratitude, and taking the opportunity to experience the beauty of nature). Incorporating these practices into your daily life requires commitment and perseverance, but it can have a significant effect on your mental and physical health.

In conclusion, there are many techniques for practicing gratitude that can be used in your daily life. Keeping a gratitude journal, making a list of things you are grateful for, and expressing gratitude to someone directly are just some of the common techniques that can be used. Incorporating these practices into your daily life requires commitment and perseverance but can have significant effects on your mental and physical health.

How Gratitude Can Help Clear Your Mind

Gratitude not only helps you focus on the positives in life; it can also help you reduce stress and anxiety by clearing your mind of negative thoughts. Instead of focusing on your problems and worries, gratitude helps you see things more positively and appreciate the things you have in life.

When we feel stressed or anxious, we often focus on problems and negative thoughts, which can make the situation worse. Gratitude helps us break this negative thought cycle and focus on what is positive in our lives. This can reduce stress and anxiety, helping us to feel calmer and more peaceful.

Gratitude can also help develop mindfulness and awareness of the present moment. When we are grateful, we are more present in the present moment and less inclined to worry about the past or future. This helps us focus on the activities we are doing and fully enjoy the happy moments in life.

In addition, gratitude can help develop a greater awareness of one's emotions. When we are grateful, we are more aware of the positive emotions we are experiencing and the sources that generated them. This awareness helps us develop a greater understanding of ourselves and our emotions, which can help improve our mental health.

Finally, it is important to remember that gratitude should not be used to deny your negative feelings. It is normal to occasionally feel sad, angry, or frustrated, and gratitude should not be used to ignore these feelings; instead, gratitude should be used to help empty your mind and focus on the positive aspects of life—even when things seem difficult or complex.

The Powerful Impact of Gratitude on Mental Health

The power of gratitude for mental health has been the subject of much scientific research in recent decades. Gratitude can be defined as a mental state of appreciation for positive things in life, such as relationships, experiences and personal resources. The practice of gratitude can bring many benefits to mental health, including improved mood, resilience and happiness.

A study conducted by Emmons and McCullough in 2003 showed that gratitude practice can improve mood and reduce symptoms of depression. Study participants who kept a daily gratitude journal reported a significant improvement in their psychological well-being compared with the control group.

Another study conducted by Wood, Joseph and Maltby in 2009 explored the link between gratitude and emotional resilience. Participants who reported a high level of gratitude showed greater resilience and ability to overcome obstacles in life than those with a low level of gratitude.

In addition, a study conducted by Lyubomirsky, Sheldon and Schkade in 2005 showed that gratitude practice can increase levels of happiness and overall well-being. Study participants who kept a weekly gratitude journal reported a significant increase in their levels of happiness and life satisfaction compared to the control group.

In summary, gratitude is an important adaptive skill that can bring many benefits to mental health. Practicing gratitude can improve mood, emotional resilience and happiness. Gratitude can be practiced in many ways, such as keeping a gratitude journal, expressing gratitude to friends and family, or simply focusing on positive moments in daily life.

How to Integrate Gratitude into Your Daily life

Incorporating gratitude into daily life is an important habit that can bring many benefits to mental health. There are many activities that can help increase feelings of gratitude and appreciation in everyday life.

The following are some suggestions on how to incorporate gratitude into your life:

• **Keeping a Gratitude Journal:** Gratitude journaling is a simple but powerful practice to increase gratitude in your daily life. Take a few minutes each day to write down at least three things for which you are grateful. This can help you focus on the positive moments in your life and appreciate the little things you often take for granted.

• **Express Gratitude to Friends and Family**: Expressing gratitude to those around us is an excellent habit. Take time to thank the important people in your life. You can do this verbally or write them a thank-you note.

• **Integrating Gratitude into Exercise:** Exercise is an excellent opportunity to practice gratitude. As you exercise, try to focus on your successes, and the progress you have made. Appreciate your body, and its ability to move and exercise.

• **Practicing Gratitude Meditation:** Meditation is an excellent practice to increase gratitude in your daily life. Take a few minutes each day to meditate on your feelings of gratitude. Focus on the positive moments in your life. There are many apps that offer guided meditations on gratitude.

• **Bring Gratitude into Your Daily Routine:** Try to incorporate gratitude into your daily routine. For example, when you wake up in the morning, take a few minutes to think about what you are grateful for. Whenever you eat, take time to appreciate the food, and the person who prepared it (even if it was you!). Take time each day to focus on the positive moments in your life.

Turning Gratitude into a Habit

Gratitude is a powerful emotion that can have a significant impact on our lives and happiness. While it can be easy to feel gratitude for big things in life, such as success or positive relationships, it can be more difficult to feel gratitude for small, everyday things. However, the regular practice of gratitude can help create lasting change in your life.

Gratitude can become a habitual part of your life, just like other daily activities like taking out the trash or drinking your morning coffee. You can start with small steps, such as taking a moment each day to reflect on what you are grateful for. You can also keep a gratitude journal, writing a list of things you are grateful for each day. This practice can help you develop a more positive mindset and focus on the positive things in your life.

While gratitude may seem like a simple practice, it can have profound effects on your life. It can help you develop more positive relationships with others and find more joy in the little things. In addition, gratitude can help you manage stress and anxiety, as it helps you focus on your successes and strengths.

To make gratitude a habitual part of your life, it can be helpful to create a daily routine. For example, you can start your day by writing in your gratitude journal or taking a moment to reflect on what you are grateful for while brushing your teeth. You can also incorporate gratitude into your social interactions, such as expressing your gratitude toward others when they do something kind for you.

In general, the regular practice of gratitude can help create lasting change in your life. It can help you develop a more positive mindset and focus on the positive things in your life, which can lead to more positive relationships, greater happiness and less stress. Start with small steps and create a daily routine to develop gratitude as a habit in your life.

The power of gratitude can be used as a tool to empty the mind on command. We live in an increasingly hectic and stressful world, where worries and anxieties can easily suffocate the mind. Regular practice of gratitude can help create space in the mind to focus on the positive moments in life, helping to reduce stress and anxiety.

In addition, gratitude can also contribute to the overall well-being of a person's life. When we are grateful for what we have in life, we are more likely to feel happy and satisfied. Gratitude can also help develop positive relationships with others, creating a sense of connection and mutual appreciation.

Finally, gratitude is a practice that can be developed and cultivated over time. It may take time and energy to develop a regular habit of gratitude, but the long-term benefits can be significant. It can be helpful to start with small steps, such as taking a moment each day to reflect on what you are grateful for, and then incorporating gratitude into your daily routine.

In summary, gratitude is a powerful tool for emptying the mind on command. It can help clear the mind of worries and stress, creating a space to focus on the positive moments in life. Gratitude can also contribute to the overall well-being of a person's life, helping to develop positive relationships and a happier, more satisfied mindset. Start developing the practice of gratitude today and discover how it can improve your life.

Chapter 13.
The Gratitude Journal

In this final chapter we focus attention on the good things in life, even small things, for which to be grateful.

Here is an example of what a gratitude journal might look like:

Every night before you go to sleep, take a few minutes to reflect on the positive moments of the day and the things you are grateful for. Write down three things you are grateful for at that moment and try to focus on even small, but meaningful things.

For example:
• I am grateful for the sunshine that warmed me today as I walked to the office.
• I am grateful for having a good conversation with a colleague today.
• I am grateful for having dinner with my family and the time spent together.

Start with just three things and, if you wish, increase the number over time. The gratitude journal is a simple but effective way to focus attention on the good things in life, even the smallest things, and to develop the practice of gratitude.

Below you can write down the good things in your life, as outlined in this chapter.

_____

_____

Conclusion

In conclusion, keeping your mind free from negative and disempowering thoughts is an attainable and fundamental goal that will help you live a peaceful and happy life. This book offers a variety of tools and techniques (e.g., meditation, gratitude, physical activity, and self-compassion) that will help you achieve this goal.

One of the main themes of the book was the power of positive thinking. This does not mean that one should ignore the reality of difficult times in life, but rather it is about always looking for the positive side of things and developing a positive mindset.

In addition, the book emphasized the importance of finding activities and passions that bring joy to life, such as cultivating positive relationships with others and engaging in creative projects. These factors can help create a fulfilling and meaningful life.

Finally, it is important to emphasize that maintaining a mind free of negative thoughts requires constant effort and regular practice. There will always be difficult times in life, but the important thing is to develop the mental and behavioral habits that will help us overcome these challenges with strength and resilience.

In summary, this book has provided practical tools and techniques to help you free your mind from negative and disempowering thoughts, as well as improve your mental health, well-being, and quality of life. With consistent practice, these tools can be used to build a happy and fulfilling life, in which inner peace is the norm and not the exception.

YOUR FREE GIFTS!

SCAN ME

GIFT #1
AudioTrack

**VISUALIZATIONS
TO FIND INNER PEACE**

GIFT #2
AudioTrack

**AFFIRMATIONS TO OVERCOME
ANXIETY AND EMOTIONAL SCARS**

SCAN ME

SCAN ME

GIFT #3
AudioTrack

**MEDITATION FOR LIVING IN THE
PRESENT MOMENT (HERE AND NOW)**

GIFT #4
AudioTrack

**HYPNOSIS TO CLEAR YOUR MIND OF
NEGATIVE THINKING AND WORRIES**

SCAN ME

Made in the USA
Middletown, DE
18 August 2023

36921484R00064